Born Feisty

How a Near Death Experience & a suicide gave me a sense of purpose and a message for our time

Danica Apolline

First Published in Great Britain in 2019 by Danica Apolline

978-0-9575721-6-4

www.danicaapolline.co.uk

The information given in this book should not be treated as a substitute for professional medical advice; always consult a medical practitioner. Any use of information in this book is at the reader's discretion and risk. The author cannot be held responsible for any loss, claim or damage arising out of the use, or misuse of any key of this book or the suggestions made or the failure to take medical advice.

Other books by Danica Apolline

The Spiritual Teachers' Handbook

Nature's Medicine Code

Online Programs by Danica Apolline

The Spiritual Teachers' Program

The Changemakers' Program

To each and every soul with whom I have shared a moment where we have laughed, cried, danced, been wowed and lived.

And to Keith Flint. Bet the raves in heaven are amazing now you're there.

"Here is the test to find whether or not your mission on earth is finished: If you are alive, it isn't."

~ Richard Bach

Introduction

As I sit writing this, I am looking back at a few truly profound weeks in my life.

It is a month since Keith Flint aka "The Firestarter" from The Prodigy, my favourite band, hanged himself.

I had – up until this point - never really quite understood why fans get really upset and cry when their favourite musicians die. Now I get it. The Prodigy were the soundtrack to my life, especially to my teenage years, Out of Space is in my will to be played at my funeral, and it is not exaggeration to say that their music, and the rave scene literally saved me. Well, them and some angels we will meet in a bit.

My early life was extremely hard........yet I would hear their tunes and I was transported to a heaven on earth that kept me alive, breathing, thriving, connected and happy. I felt and knew love - without taking the drugs back then - through their tunes and other old school raving classics. But it was theirs that always blew me away the most.

The gratitude in my heart this last month has been massive. The sadness I have been feeling has been massive too.

Keith's passing has stirred something else up in me. I have been seeing an anger that has taken me by surprise. A memory awakened.

I am usually the first to respect people's right to live in a way that fits them, as long as it doesn't hurt others. I also am usually the first to respect people's right to die as they choose (again without endangering the lives of others). This is the first time I have struggled, because I know he could have been persuaded to come back, and I wish he had been.

I have been remembering the journey I made when I hung myself too. But I wasn't allowed through to "the other side". I was persuaded to come back.

This is a book about what happened.

Before I go any further, I'd like to tell you something. What happened was so beautiful and amazing, I will try my best to describe it with words, and my wish is that your hearts and imaginations can experience even an iota of the wonder of it all. But what led me to that point wasn't wonderful, some of which I will share. You might need some tissues. But what happened in my life isn't who I am, in the same way that your life experiences aren't who you are.

As you read this journey, know that I am a happy person, positive and an optimist. That's probably what's helped me be here now.

I live a happy life as an author, speaker, healer, teacher of healing, Strengthscope trainer and facilitator, occasional baker of healthy vegan, organic, free from cakes having started the Conscious Cake Company and am a health visionary. I am studying to become a homeopath, having always been fascinated by medicine, as you will find out from this book. I have a truly wonderful son and am happy as a mama. I am blessed to have some truly remarkable brilliant friends.

I laugh deeply, and loudly, and have a wicked sense of fun and humour. People are funny to me – and the smallest things make me smile. Acts of kindness, people being themselves – you know, those people who dance on the tube to their tunes like no-one is watching. I LOVE those people. In fact I AM one of those people. I love a great festival, dancing, singing, I don't give a fuck that I don't have the booty and beauty of Beyonce or the voice of Pink or Adele, I still SING. And dance. And move. And live.

So even though the story I share is about a death, and about some of the sad and painful journey to it, this book - more than anything - is about the wonder and magic of life, and how in being here, we have a purpose......and about making it through really tough times to finding peace and happiness.

I am strong. I have walked through fire and pain and anguish and abuse. But I don't carry baggage. Like a caterpillar in a chrysalis, I have taken every moment and transformed it into a beautiful colourful gift that I hope is helpful to others who would also like to let go of their baggage so they can also live life and be free.

So as I share the painful stuff, know that it's just to give you a context, to help you understand how and why I got to making the choice I made to die. And if you hold on through that, and keep reading, you'll get to find out about the wonder that I found when I did.

It's probably a good time to go and get a nice cup of tea.

1

I wrote this when I was 21 years old.

"My name is Danica Matic (pronounced Da-ni-tsa Ma-tich), Danica being the name of the morning star, apparently. If so, my Mum must have a sick sense of humour 'cos I hate mornings. In fact I don't even begin to wake up until 8 o'clock in the evening.

I am of a chubby-ish build, the chubby-ness mainly owning to the elephant-bearing hips that I possess. I wear round tortoiseshell glasses that are constantly slipping off my nose, so I am often seen pushing them back into place like mad old professors seem to. I have very long, straight brown hair and greeny-grey eyes that smile, apparently. I am always smiling, irrespective of whether I am happy or sad, which people seem to find endearing – and deceiving. I am generally a nice, warm, caring, friendly, happy-smiley person who talks and laughs much too loudly. I want to be "everybody's mum", much to the annoyance of many. I regularly break other people's possessions completely by accident because I am very clumsy, usually by knocking them over with my hips. As a work friend once observed: "Can't you go and have an operation or something for those things?!". I think I can be self-centred and exhibitionist at times, but my housemate, Simon, disagrees.

I am 21 years old, going on 60.

I try to explain this to people who don't understand; friends, my psychiatrist, my Mum, but I feel old, and tired of all of the pain. Perhaps the smile hides it from them too well.

I feel like a swimmer who is swimming the English Channel. The sea is cold and raging, and I am fighting against the wind, rain, and waves to complete those 26 miles when I can touch the French coast; my destination. It is a long, hard journey, so I pace myself. I can eventually see the French coast ahead of me, and even though I am exhausted and each stroke is more painful than the last, I look forward to reaching my destination, for I know I will have accomplished something tremendous. Just as I reach for the coastline, with my last iota of strength, it moves back 10 yards – nothing compared with how far I have come – but enough for me to feel the power of the elements overcome me. No-one can hear my cries: "Help me. I'm drowning.". "

~

Shortly after I wrote this, I killed myself. I hung myself from some rafters at a shelter in Platt Fields Park in Manchester. I made two attempts to sit down whilst attached by a long piece of material to the rafters before the third and final attempt. The first two were painful and scary, so I stood up again before coming to "the end". The third time however, I stayed down. I went past the pain. In fact, once the pain stopped, it felt amazing. Truly, deeply, profoundly wonderful. I saw a bright Light that spun above me and felt a peace unlike anything that I had ever even come close to in my life. I surrendered to that light and to that incredible peace.

The next thing I knew, I found myself standing, breathing, alive. I still don't know how it happened.

I do believe that I lost time. I don't know how much to be precise; I didn't exactly record my "Time of Death". I do know that when I found myself standing on my feet, it was a while later. How do I know? I felt it somehow....maybe the sky was darker, maybe the temperature was colder, I still can't explain it......more than anything it was a feeling, just an inner knowing that something had happened and the time I was now standing in was not just a couple of minutes after I had been sitting down. It was definitely Later.

I felt as though I was being gently guided back out of the park, in a haze. You know how when a little toddler toddles around, and looks like they are going to toddle their way into a wall, or to an oven, or somewhere else dangerous like that, and a loving parent just steers them away, and off they go, toddling off in a new direction without any change of pace, or indeed realizing that their direction has changed? Well that was how I felt. Like I was being gently guided with loving arms around my shoulders, as though I was being encouraged to toddle off in a new direction – out of the park.

Even though it was pitch dark as I walked out of Platt Fields, my attention was drawn to something unusual along the path. It was – as I later described to my therapist – "a mutant daffodil"; it had two heads. One head was dying, old and withered. The other was bright, alive and full of hope.

I spent many years wondering what had happened in that "lost time". I looked forward to the day when I would find out – I supposed it would take me dying again for that to happen. But then, many years later, I spontaneously travelled back to that time in meditation and was shown some of what occurred. I subsequently travelled back two more times in meditation, to be shown all of what I share in this book.

But before I tell you about what I was shown, I think some context might be helpful. I think I need to tell you a little bit about how I got to that evening in Platt Fields. It wasn't a rash decision, it wasn't even a desperate one, but one that actually in the end (pun intended) brought me a huge peacefulness.

2

I was born and raised in London, the first child of Yugoslav immigrants. My mother and father met in London, at the Serbian Community Centre in Ladbroke Grove. It is on a street just off the super trendy Portobello Road, which has always felt like a wonderful irony to me. The Community Centre is a 1970's style building, a bit out of place tagged on the side of the beautiful Serbian Orthodox Church next to it. It has only been re-decorated twice in all my 35 years, and seems to perfectly reflect the older members of the community who came over when Serbia was part of a communist Yugoslavia. Tito, Yugoslavia's communist leader, would probably have felt most at home there in the décor – even if he would have been unwelcome by the community, most of whom were Royalists who left Yugoslavia to escape their experiences of being oppressed under communism.

When my Mum planned to leave Yugoslavia, she had originally meant to fly to Germany to be an au pair. Her ticket had been booked, the family arranged, the goodbyes said. Yet, for some reason that she could never explain, she changed her mind at the last minute. Apparently everything in her just said "no!". Given how desperate she was to leave, it must have been a pretty strong feeling. She would tell me how the plane she was due to fly on crashed and everyone on it died. I checked this out, many years after her death, and it turned out that there had in fact been a plane crash; it appears that the plane she was due to fly on crashed on its journey from Germany to Yugoslavia – I guess she was booked on a flight that never could have been made because the plane never got to Yugoslavia to collect her.

She decided instead to come to England. It was 1972. She was a "legal alien" under the Aliens Order 1953. She had to carry a Certificate of Registration – a pass card that I still keep – that she was required to show to any police or immigration officer that asked for it. She worked as a domestic in a range of hotels in the Paddington area.

She lived with her cousin and her cousin's husband, Čika Perica (pronounced Chika Peritsa, which means Uncle Peter), when she first arrived. Čika Perica who has a wonderful sense of humour, decided he'd "help" my Mum by teaching her some of the customs he said that we had here in England. My Mum was working on Christmas Day during her first winter here, and hadn't been here long, so still hadn't learned a lot of English. There was, of course, no public transport my Mum could use to get to work that day, so she was reliant on using taxis.

"The taxi drivers here in England do something wonderful for people on Christmas Day", my Uncle had said. "They insist that no-one give them a tip, because they know how hard it must be for workers to have to work, so it's their way of giving back to the workers". He didn't stop there.

"The English for "Happy Christmas", which you must say to the taxi driver, is "Fuck off"".

My Mum always laughed telling this story, and how confused she was that first English Christmas Day, seeing the taxi driver shouting at her, and waving his arms in an angry fashion. She had after all followed my Uncle's instructions perfectly!

She met my father a couple of years later. They had been going out for 4 months when my mother fell pregnant with me. She was desperate to have a child, and so was "a bit careless" apparently. My feelings around this ended up being one of my life's lessons....I was angry and unforgiving of my Mum for years for this.....I blamed what I felt was her carelessness for my experiences as a child. In my later teen angst, I felt that I had been brought into a life that "wasn't planned"; that "I didn't ask for; that I didn't want".

I arrived at, what I now believe, was the perfect time for me - a month premature. In those days, this meant 3 weeks in an incubator (or a "fish tank" as I like to call them). My Mum had pre-eclampsia, and the umbilical cord was wrapped around my neck. I often wonder if I was trying to hang myself, knowing what awaited me, even back then. She went into hospital for a scan as an outpatient, and was told that she would be having me that day. It turns out my arrival was an emergency. I was born by Caesarean at 5.31pm. My Mum's English was still not very good, and I believe she didn't really understand what was happening, and was totally traumatised by the whole experience. Despite being desperate to have me, she didn't see me for the first 3 days of my life. Not because of any complications, but because she had been traumatised by the experience and just wasn't coping. Eventually she allowed herself to be persuaded by the midwives to be wheeled to the nursery. Back in Yugoslavia, it was still common for children to be accidentally swapped in hospitals, which was a fear for my Mum. She said she always knew I was hers when she saw me; I had the same tiny beads of sweat on my nose that she would get when she was hot too.

She named me Danica, meaning morning star; the Yugolav, or Serbian, name for Venus.

I was 15 years old before I saw a full length photo of my parents on their wedding day. My mother was obviously heavily pregnant! I must have said this out loud, when going through some photo albums with my cousin Olga. Olga just started laughing and said "didn't you know?!". My mum just laughed later when I had a go at her for being so strict with me – for not allowing me to go out, for making it hard for me to hang out with friends, for not allowing me to have boyfriends (until I was "married to them") – and here she was, pregnant with me before she got married!

Many years later, when I returned home from university, following my mother's diagnosis of lung cancer, I became quickly fond of her best friend's daily visits for cups of coffee. Tetka ("Auntie" in Serbian) Ljubica lived on the same road, so was always popping in and out, and they would both hang out with me, asking me when I would make my mum a grandmother. "I don't even have a boyfriend......" I would remind them. After about 3 weeks of this daily pestering, I had a moment of revelation that still tickles me now. I shared this with my Mum. She was – as I almost always remember her – standing at the cooker, making yet another cup of strong Turkish coffee, whilst I sat on a stool in the kitchen. It was my favourite place for us to talk and chat and hang out. We were yapping about everyday things when I gently turned the conversation to another subject altogether. "Mum?", I began. "If I came home tomorrow, and told you that I was not only pregnant, but that I didn't even know who the father was......you wouldn't care, would you?" My – at times - very strict mama turned to me, smiling a lovely smile that showed she thought it was funny that she'd been – yet again - caught out and replied "no I wouldn't.......but if you tell anyone, I'll deny it!".

My life, on a good day, was very much like something out of the film "My Big Fat Greek Wedding" – I had a connection to both the British and Serbian cultures. However I never completely fitted into either – or indeed ever felt comfortable in either. I was considered to be too "English" in my politeness and quietness and ability to listen by the Serbs, and too "Serbian" by my English friends, who thought me loud, overly direct and blunt and unsubtle. I never felt at home anywhere.....and I had this yearning to find it.

3

I went to an ordinary local primary school and I loved it. I loved learning. I was good at it. I was the second tallest in my class – tallest girl in fact. I can't remember which of the lads it was that was taller than me. I think this was the first place that I started being asked to teach others. I happened to be top of the class along with Dominic. It was Mrs Double, our PE teacher, who I remember first asking me to help others to learn – helping some of the struggling kids in my class to understand our biology lesson. Mrs Double was a funny lady. She was very loud and direct, and scary; she would shout quite a lot. And she would wear thin light pink towelling tracksuit bottoms with open toe sandals, even though she looked very old to me. I would be able to see the print of her knickers through the tracksuit bottoms. I always wondered whether she knew that we could see the stripes, or the butterflies that would come through. For all her scariness, she knew I understood what we were learning, and it made me feel good to be able to help. To give. To be recognised and valued. To feel like I mattered in some way. In school, I was safe.

I was always well behaved too. Apart from 3 occasions I can remember.

The first was when I was about 7, and I was playing "Witches" with Claire Reynolds. My favourite thing to do at playtime was to dance with Corey and Amanda and all the cool kids to Fame. We had developed our own routine, and we really did feel like we were "learning to fly....high". I don't remember how I ended up playing with Claire instead, but as she was explaining the instructions, I was too busy paying attention to Corey (an amazing dancer, who lived in a care home) and co, and wishing I was dancing too. What Claire had been explaining was that she would be the "witch" and she would catch me and put me in her cauldron. Because I hadn't been listening, I had no idea why suddenly she was strangling me. I really thought she was trying to kill me. Or maybe I was scared that she was, because I knew that feeling from home. So I did the only thing I could in that moment to defend myself. I bit the nearest part of her body to me. It happened to be her cheek. And I was too scared to let go. Bless her heart, her cheek swelled up and stayed that way for 3 days, and she had teeth marks in her face for a week. I had never heard English swearing before her mother saw me at the end of the day. I remember asking my mum what "fuck" meant. I think she'd learned by that point, even though she didn't tell me.

The second was in Mr Kiely's class. He was such an inspirational teacher. He was my form tutor when I was 10. He was very kindly towards us all, and fun-loving too. He made me feel safe in a way I hadn't felt in the presence of a grown-up man before, and it made me feel uncomfortable to be honest. I didn't know how to deal with it, so I think I developed some sort of an early crush on him. I remember showing him some of my work for him to check when we were learning biology, and he used the word "body" and I felt embarrassed and ashamed. My father had brought me up to be ashamed of my body, and that it was a dirty sexual thing, and I equated "body" with "sex" and "wrong" for some time. Mr Kiely used to give us the best Friday afternoon quizzes; we all loved them because he used to dress them up as though they were exciting game shows.

So one day, Imran, a boy in my class, spotted that I was chewing gum. Illegally. He put his hand up and said "Sir! Sir! Danica's chewing gum". I think this confused Mr Kiely because I was considered to be such a well-behaved child. I said "no I'm not", and then did this bizarre putting-my-hand-over-my-mouth-spitting-out-the-gum-into-hand-so-no-one-would-see type manoeuvre. And then panicked because I had this illegal contraband in my hand, and could get caught. So I "really subtly" slid my hand to the back of my neck as if was I then resting my neck and head on it, and hid my gum there. Imran saw all of this, and told Mr Kiely, who told him off for telling tales.

I spent the rest of the day struggling to bend my head fully forward because my hair got stuck to the gum. My mum gave up trying to remove it after what felt like an age of her telling me to "sit still!". The only way around it that she could think of was to chop some of my hair off. It was the only time until I was 21 that I had short hair – or indeed, went to a hairdressers..

The third time was in my first year at secondary school. Before our Maths class with Mrs Watson – a lovely kind middle-aged teacher – we were all mucking about with the whiteboards. Our classrooms had 2 sliding whiteboards. One would slide behind the other, so that if one was high and the other low, you would literally have a wall of whiteboard. We were bent under the high board, and would bring down the other board down low in front of us, so we were hiding behind it. I think Mrs Watson might have been a bit late because we lost track of time. Suddenly someone heard her coming and shouted "quick!" and everyone ran out from behind the whiteboard.....except me. I can't remember whether I it was because I was too slow, or thought it would be funny. So it turned out that Mrs Watson had forgotten her whiteboard markers, so she wasn't going to be moving the board and find me behind it. I was bent double to fit in the tiny space, and my back started to hurt. I heard the girls say I had a violin lesson when Mrs Watson went through the register and asked why I wasn't there. Why she didn't ask more questions I don't know, because my violin was blatantly sitting on my desk. After some time, the ache in my back became intolerable, so I started to push the board up very gently. In my head, I thought that if I did it really gently and quietly, maybe Mrs Watson wouldn't notice and I could just sneak past her and into my seat, as though I were invisible, and everything would be alright. But no. The board squeaked. Loudly. With every squeak, the whole class would start laughing. Mrs Watson carried on with the lesson. And it went on like this for a little while......me pushing the board up a fraction, it squeaking, the class laughing, Mrs Watson carrying on with the lesson. Eventually, I pushed up the board, and stepped forward. The class was in hysterics by now. They did all go into a hushed silence as Mrs Watson went to speak. She looked at me, smiling, and told me that I had 10 seconds to get out of the classroom. I didn't know if she was joking or not because of her smile. So I stayed rooted to the spot. After 10 seconds, she took me to the library and told me to see her at lunchtime. At lunchtime, she told me I had detention after school. And then it was no longer funny. My father was supposed to be picking me up from school that day. I panicked - he would kill me. All of us say that about our parents. Not many of us mean it literally. I don't know how I persuaded Mrs Watson to let me off, but I do remember the sheer relief of realising that I had avoided a fate worse than death. The torture before it.

4

I know that my father didn't want a child. And then when I was born a girl rather than a boy, that made him very angry - at both my mum and at me. Then, to top things off, I was a girl with principles and I knew that his behaviour was not loving or kind. I wasn't always afraid to show him and tell him and challenge him to see that, especially when I was really small. I was born with spirit. I was feisty.

My earliest memory is of standing – in a nappy – between my parents who are arguing. I told my father to stop being horrible to mummy and my mummy to stop shouting at daddy. Even now, I am stunned that I ever had the courage (or was it defiance?) to do that, as I will already have seen my father was like, and will have known I had put myself and my mother in danger.

My earliest full memory of him probably summarises my experiences of him in my life perfectly. We were on holiday in Yugoslavia, visiting his father and step mother. They owned a farm, and he was part of a huge family, many of whom still worked on the farm. One day, I was bored. I don't know where my brother was, and everyone was working, and so I had no-one to play with. I must have been maybe just 3 years old. So I started whining. My father came over to me and told me to shut up and then returned to work. But I still didn't have anyone to play with and I was still bored, so I carried on whining. I couldn't have imagined what my father's response would have been – I would have hoped for someone to play with, but I experienced something altogether different.

My father called over all of the members of his family who were within earshot. There must have been about 12 adults there. They all stood in a semicircle, watching as my father picked me up horizontally and then purposely dropped me onto the ground. Now it was only maybe 3-4 feet, but for a 3 year old, that is a long way down. It would be like dropping an adult, horizontally, from 12 feet. I landed hard on the ground, and was – I later realised – winded. But I didn't know what was happening, all I knew was that I was in agonising pain and couldn't breathe, and I believed I was about to die. As if that wasn't painful enough for me, my father then forbade anyone to speak to me. I went up to 4 different adults and pleaded through my sobs to know where my mother was. Each one literally turned their backs to me and walked away. That was the moment in my life when I think I broke. When I eventually found my mother, she was sitting at a sewing machine, and she was whispering so no one could hear, pleading with me to go away, fighting back tears, whilst I begged her to hold me, to make the pain go away, to save me from dying. I only ever saw my Mum cry 3 times in my life. I could see and feel that she was scared so I did as she asked, but she was looking into my eyes with so much love – as if that was the only way she could safely communicate to me that she loved me and that I would be OK.

Many years later, when we cancelled a trip to Yugoslavia because we found out my father had arranged to kill her there, I understood that here – with his family in a rural backwater of East Europe – she had no voice and no support. Many people may judge that what my mother did was cruel – but I believe in that moment she was doing everything she could to keep us alive.

I was with my father the day that he bought the gun that I believe he planned to kill my mother with on that trip to Yugoslavia that my Mum cancelled, once we found out his plans to kill her there. I would have been maybe 8 years old. When I realised that he was buying a gun, and had this horrendous gut-wrenching dread that it was to be used on my Mum, I asked if I could go and sit in the car, so that I could hide from him the tears and the terror I felt. I sat in the car and sobbed and sobbed until he returned, when I had to immediately turn the tears and the emotions off to keep us all safe.

My parents had just divorced – I think I was one of the few children in the world that was truly happy, joyful and celebratory when my parents split up. When I visited my father at his house in a small place called Greenford, he would tell me about this other woman who would look after me and be my new mum, once we went on this trip to Yugoslavia. I asked him why I needed a new one – what was going to happen to my mum? He never answered that question. He would use these chats as an opportunity to tell me that there was something wrong with my mother – she was ill in the head. On one occasion, I decided I didn't need to listen to it anymore. He refused to take me home as I had asked, so I got up, put my shoes on, and walked out of his house. I felt strong and stubborn as I started on my long walk home. I was going to get myself there all by myself, without him, on foot. All 6 miles of them with my little 8 years old legs, along the M40 dual carriageway – a motorway. After about 10 minutes, he pulled up his car alongside me and angrily told me to get in the car so he could drive me home. I was scared to at first, and still feeling defiant. But I could see something different in him in that moment. I don't know what it was that softened him, maybe seeing my strength, or stubbornness, a familiar family and Serbian trait – or indeed my feisty spirit. But I felt and trusted that this wouldn't be the time he would try to kill me so I got in the car eventually and let him drive me home.

Unfortunately for me, my parents didn't stay apart, and kept getting back together and splitting up until I was 15 years old. My little sister was born when I was 11 years old. Even after the age of 15, he would still follow me, and come and find me, so I never felt truly safe. At the age of 17, he came and found me one lunch time from work, and because I refused to do what he was telling me to, punched me full in the face.

The bit I remember the most about the time that he threw a huge concrete paving slab at my mother's head – she miraculously escaped with just a graze – is not the actual moment of violence. It is the moment I was standing in a hospital cubicle with my mum, and she was bending over, ready to be given a tetanus jab in hospital, and in my own little 7-year old way, thinking "when I grow up, I hope my bum isn't as big as that". Had the slab hit my mother with the full force and the direction my father threw it, it would definitely have left her very seriously brain damaged or dead. I saw an angel push her out of the way.

There were only a few times that my father was actually violent, but when he was, it was terrifying – and usually life-threatening. He literally pasted my skull against a wall when I didn't tie my shoelaces up quickly enough one morning. We were running late to leave the house. I was only young, and had only just learned how to do them up, so was slow.

The only time my mother intervened was when I was 15 years old, and he had been chasing me around the dining room table poised to stab me with my mother's heavy duty tailoring scissors. They were 10 inches long. He had asked me a question, and I had replied, in a way that I thought was without any emotion. He thought I had done so rudely, and that was – in his mind – reason enough to kill me. I genuinely thought I was going to die, and prepared myself for it. I was cowering on the floor, holding up a dining chair above me to protect myself. My Mum must have known that This Was It, which I feel was why she stepped in. Interestingly, the only time he ever apologised to me for his behaviour whilst sober was a few days after this. His way of saying sorry was to give me £100 to get myself something nice.

He was also completely obsessed with my sexuality – or to be more precise – my virginity. It was very important to him that I remain a virgin until I was married. He thought it appropriate to tell me that I was not allowed to use tampons for this reason, and tried to arrange a marriage for me when I was 14 years old. He didn't feel education was necessary for a girl, as my only job should have been knowing how to look after my husband.

When I was 8 years old, my mother had her first full psychotic breakdown, the first of a series of psychoses that were part of her being diagnosed with bipolar affective disorder. She was taken to an old psychiatric hospital – like something out of "One Flew Over The Cuckoos Nest", where she remained for a month. She came out a bit mentally fried from the Electric Shock Treatment, antipsychotics and tranquilisers. I found this a really hard time, but I knew I had to be strong for my Mum so that I could help her. I knew her spirit was still in there, that the drugs hadn't taken her away completely, although she really was quite cabbaged. I still remember the smiling but sad glint of recognition in her eye when I took her some of the jam tarts that I had learned to make at school, and then made especially for her at home, so I could take them to her in hospital. It was the only thing I could think of to do to try to give her something to help make her better. Again my feisty spirit showed itself, as my father got annoyed at the mess I was making in the kitchen, and wondered why I was bothering. But I refused to listen, and was determined to take her something that I hoped could help her feel better.

These were my first attempt at cooking, and I wanted to share them with her. I remember pouring all my love into them, all my wishes that they would make her better. Many years later when I accidentally started a vegan, organic free from cake business, I realised that my commitment to blessing food with love, wishing that my food bring people health and happiness started here.

It was during this time my mother was in hospital that my father, whilst giving me a shower one day, decided to be more intimate in his cleaning of me.

The way my father most challenged me was through his unpredictability. He was hugely unpredictable, and all the time. He wasn't violent when he was drunk – he was violent sober. In fact, the only times I could predict I was safe with him was when he was drunk, he was actually a lovely drunk. Unfortunately he didn't drink much. There was a time when he was drunk that I told him he could be really horrible to us, and he smiled at me, and said "I know", then got out his wallet and gave me a £50 note "to buy something nice".

His pathological violence when sober led me in later years to wonder if he was a psychopath. I remember being stunned, during a lecture on psychopathy when I was studying for my psychology degree, that I could easily tick 13 out of 20 characteristics for him on a psychopathy questionnaire – that was without taking the time to think about the questions. 14 was the score that determined a psychopath. I am sure had I taken the time to think about the questions, in between listening to the lecturer, he would have had the 14.

I could see the flashing dance of danger in his eyes in every moment, and I had to keep myself safe from its explosion. He would regularly ask me random questions that required a definite 1-word answer, like "do you think people who use drugs should go to prison?". He would already have decided what he felt the right answer should be, and the test was whether I could give the same answer as him or not, and if I got it wrong.....well, it was like playing Russian Roulette. I kind of developed a way of reading his mind, or feeling for the right answer – of listening to my intuition - to keep myself safe.

So what I actually lived with – more than the violence itself – was the fear of what was to come. Actually, it was more than fear, it was *terror.* My Mum and I knew what he was capable of. It is the terror that was damaging. Not the bruises, not the wounds. And it was always there, so school was my sanctuary. Even when I was out and about, I knew I wasn't safe. He would follow me sometimes to find out what I was doing. I caught him at it once, so the only true safety I knew was school. I was going to do my best to make sure I could be in it all the time by doing well.

The physical violence when it did happen was rare, but life-threatening, and began whilst I was still in my mother's womb. Even though the actual violence didn't happen continuously, the *threat* of it was with us 24 hours a day, 7 days a week, 365 days a year. So I lived in terror for the first 15 years of my life until he finally left. It didn't end then – but it stopped being constant. He also spent 20 years visiting African witch doctors and witches from other cultures – as well as practicing black magic himself - putting curses on all of us. This is something that is taboo in British culture to talk about, but in the culture of my parents? Everyone knew the "village witch", who could and would put curses on people you didn't like for a price. He learned the art from his delightful step-mother. Living in England didn't change this, I always knew who the witches in our community were. It doesn't matter whether or not you believe in curses, the fact that someone is willing to carry them out on another person, and tries to do so, is spiritual abuse.

Nobody asked why I was still wetting the bed when I was 11 years old, ashamed and embarrassed that my body wasn't able to do what it was supposed to while I slept.

To me, he was my Darth Vader. I LOVE Star Wars. LOVE LOVE LOVE it. I remember as a child watching the films and feeling so much resonance with the story of Luke and his father. There is a scene at the end of Return of The Jedi when Luke Skywalker removes the mask of his father, and tells his father that he wants to save him. "You already have" is the last thing that Anakin Skywalker says to Luke before he dies. I felt that so deeply in my heart as a story I would come to know; a story I already knew, and lived and understood.

I look back at the anger I had at my life, and yet I didn't direct my anger at my father (that would've got me killed), but unfairly at my mother instead. I directed my anger at her, not him, because even as a small child, I knew he couldn't help it. I knew deep down that there was a beautiful soul somewhere in there, but there was something else that had taken over. I only remember experiencing kindness from my father on a couple of occasions, but I always felt like I had seen a kinder soul somewhere – it was like seeing a small beautiful kind boy that had become lost and couldn't find his way out. My mother on the other hand, was bright – despite her lack of education – witty, funny, insightful, wise, clever and....I felt for many years, Should Have Known Better. Life has taught me how wrong I was, and how worthy of compassion she was.

Yet something amazing happened with my relationship with my father, many years after I had tried to kill myself for the final time that day in Platt Fields.

Whilst running one of my healing courses, I experienced a wonderful revelation in meditation. I could see what I had learned about myself through his actions. I saw that my father was one of my greatest teachers. Through his actions, I had learned that I am strong, and compassionate, and capable of surviving anything, and many other things. He had helped me – inadvertently, despite his conscious desire to keep me uneducated – to get a good education, because school was a place of safety and I did well because of my desire to be in it.

Just after I had come to understand this fully, my friend Claire came to stay. She asked me if I had seen a book that she was reading. She left it with me to read before going to bed when she stayed over. It is called *Little Soul and the Sun*. I hope that the author, Neale Donald Walsh, forgives this simplistic summary of his tremendous offering – one I fully recommend for anyone of any age.

Little Soul and the Sun is a wonderful children's book that tells the story of Little Soul. Little Soul lives in heaven and spends the beginnings of the book having a think about what he would like to be, it seems, before he begins his human life. Once he has decided, he goes to speak to God. "Can I be forgiveness?", he asks God. "Yes" says God kindly. Little Soul then wonders *how* he can be forgiveness.

At that moment, Little Soul's closest friend – another little soul – steps forward and says "I'll help you to be forgiveness.". What this other little soul offers to do is to take on all of the pain and all of the suffering that would turn him into someone who would cause Little Soul pain and suffering too. That way, Little Soul could then be what he wanted to be – forgiveness.

When I first read this book, I cried. I cried at the beauty of the story. And I cried because I knew it was true to what had happened with my father – and indeed other people with whom I had experienced pain. I knew that those with whom I had experienced great pain were in fact my greatest teachers, and the greatest and closest soul friends to me. Finally I could accept them, what they had shown me, and feel true and deep gratitude for their existence in my life.

I felt an acceptance of my experiences with my father – and a true, deep and profound peace that showed itself in the most remarkable way when it was time for him to die, again many years after that night in Platt Fields.

6

Even though I had found a peace with my father, I still knew and understood that it was not safe for me to be left alone in a room with him.

My mother, who had always insisted that I never speak badly about my father, shared with me a moment of profound recognition of how dangerous he was with me, shortly before she died.

We were sitting, watching the telly, as we did, and he came up in conversation. My Mum turned to look at me, and said very quietly, but thoughtfully, "I know you can't be left alone in a room with him." I was 24 years old.

So I always stayed far away from him. Even when I occasionally saw him at the Serbian community centre, I would move myself away. I never let him see my son, a dear friend took my baby out of the hall as soon as I saw there was a chance he would see him. There was an amazing moment, when I was dancing one of the fast moving circle dances that I grew up doing and love. One gift he gave me was the ability to dance – he himself had been a dancer in a folk dancing group alongside my dance teacher – and he loved to dance. He used to always go and dance next to the best female dancers. This was how the men in the community could court women by showing off their dancing skills, and he never stopped thinking he could do that. And then one day, he spotted a young woman dancing beautifully in the circle. She was wearing a bright pink dress, and she shone as she danced, which she always did when dancing. So he moved round to dance next to her. He went to take her hand, and she turned around to look at him, still dancing away, and he scuttled off backwards, like a spider caught in torchlight, returning to the back corner where he had been dancing. He had seen me. For the first time ever, maybe the power I had come to feel within myself startled him.

Aside from that moment, I avoided him like the plague.

So when I got a call from my wonderful friend Natasha, who I grew up with in the community, to tell me that he'd been admitted to hospital with a serious heart attack, and was in a coma, I was surprised at my response.

His heart had stopped for a whole 30 minutes before it was restarted, so he was in Intensive Care.

I went to the hospital. I *wanted* to see him. Years before, it would have been to confirm that he was dying, that I would be free of him. But my need to see him now was for different reasons.

I asked his wife if I could spend some time on my own with him, and was allowed a few minutes alone with him. As I approached his bed, a panic started to rise in me. I wondered if, in some great twist like you see in the movies, that he would suddenly open his eyes, and shoot up an arm to grab me by the throat and try to kill me. But my fearful imaginings passed quickly, and I realised he really was unconscious.

Despite being in a coma, the rage he had lived in his life was still etched on his face. But my desire to see him – my natural instinct – was just to want to be with him, to give him healing, to talk gently to help him let go and pass over if that was what he wanted; if it was his time.

"It's OK", I began saying to y father, whose name was Vidosav. I hadn't been able to call him Dad (or "Tata" as it is in Serbian) from when I was 15 years old. "You won't be met by Mum holding a celestial cricket bat" (which is what I had imagined would happen for some years after my Mum had died). "You will be met with loving open arms, and be filled with so much love. It's really beautiful, you will feel so happy there. You will have all the healing you need, and be free of all pain and suffering. It's OK to let go Vidosav, and go to the Light you can see, it's beautiful. Thank you for all you have taught me about myself. I am sorry you took on all that suffering so that I could grow. But it's a job well done. You will be met with so much love".

I could say this to him because I knew where he was going. I had already been there. This was my Luke moment. I was trying to save my Darth Vader father, I was trying to help him go towards the Light that would bring him the healing I knew he needed.

He was in a coma for 11 days before the machines were switched off. 2 days before this, I saw him appear, whilst I was in meditation. I saw his soul speak to me. It was brilliant and bright and golden and big, and so still and at peace – the complete opposite to how he had been when he was alive.

He told me he was getting ready to let go. He told me he would help me from where he was with my dreams. I kept wondering what I was looking at, because I knew his energy wasn't that of an angel, but it was as big and bright and powerful as the energies of the angels I work with.

And then I realised that, in order to help me grow so that I could make a difference and be who I am, he had to take on a personality that was full of destruction and horribleness. He could only have carried that level of destruction had he himself had a powerful soul in the first place. I recognised what some people call a" Master" – souls so powerful and brilliant and bright that they can do what the angels do and help people on the Earth, but that they have the experience of having lives on the Earth, unlike the angels.

I have come to believe that all of the people we struggle with in the world; the Donald Trumps and the Monsanto and Nestle and Big Pharma and other Corporate CEOs are all also doing the same thing. Like Luke Skywalker became a Jedi because Darth Vader existed, and like in every story with a hero, a hero only becomes a hero and shines a wonderful light in the world because the darkness calls the light to shine brightly. Now I see them as helpers, and I try as much as I can to move past my anger at how they behave. They are inviting all of us, as a humanity to RISE, bringing in a new time of love, and peace, togetherness, on the Earth. A world free of borders, where there is enough for everyone, and everyone is cared for, has a home, and a place within their community that they can make a difference to.

We can be constructive with our anger, or destructive. I believe we have a new world to build, and whilst that requires changing and getting rid of old systems that serve the few and not the whole of humanity and our planet, we can do so constructively. There are wonderful models already of this, like Citizens Assemblies and the work of Extinction Rebellion, all built around what true democracies, and non-violent protest look like.

This is the call of the darkness. It can only call to more darkness if people are afraid because the darkness grows out of fear. As Yoda so wisely said "Fear leads to anger. Anger leads to hate. Hate leads to suffering".

But darkness also calls the Light, and if people have the courage and love in their hearts to stand up and shine, no matter what the darkness does, feeling the fear and standing up for what they know is right *anyway*, then – as happens in every hero film ever made from Star Wars to Harry Potter to Lord of The Rings – the darkness ends. That is, I believe the time we are in. The darkness we see in our world is coming to an end because love and humanity are rising.

This is one of the lessons my father taught me.

7

When my mother came to the UK in 1972, she had 35p in her pocket and couldn't speak a word of English.

She had come here to escape her own story, a story I carried for her almost as though it were it were my own.

She grew up in what we would consider to be poverty in a village in Serbia – where we used to visit our grandmother Baba Dana ("Baba" means grandmother in Serbian). Even in later years, Baba Dana still had no running water in the house, or a bathroom. The toilet was an outhouse with a hole in the ground, and after a month there, I would always make a mental note not to take things for granted when I got home and had the luxury – and comfort – of a toilet seat to sit on. To have a wash in the summer, we used to shower in our swimwear by the outside standing tap that served several houses. In the winter, we used to heat up water on the wood stove in the kitchen, and then wash in the tin bath that lived under the bed in the kitchen. Our fresh drinking water would come from the well in the farm across the road – I used to love going there with Baba Dana and watching her draw up the pail of water. In the summer, we would sit and chat with my Mum who would do the washing up and washing laundry in bowls under the sweetly scented linden flower tree outside my grandmother's front door. My Mum spent years persuading her Mum to install running water and a small bathroom in her home......but never managed to persuade her to get a phone. For this, we would call the farm she worked on and we would hear the farmer's wife shouting as they ran across the road calling Baba Dana to come. "Dano! DANO! Branka na telephonu!!!" ("Dana! DANA! Branka's on the telephone!")

Baba Dana was illiterate; a peasant who worked on the land for the farmer across the road. Even in her late 70s, she could carry sacks of potatoes on her back. Funnily enough, despite never having gone to a gym (apart from an induction once when I was 18), I have always had the arm muscles of Linda Hamilton in the film Terminator.; my little joke is that I am built to carry sacks of potatoes and small grandmothers ;)

She always reminded me of Dustin Hoffman's character Raymond in Rain Man. Baba Dana had had meningitis when she was 13, and we think she had a learning disability as a result. She would walk with her head to one side like Raymond, but unlike him, she could not calculate even the most basic maths. My mother suspected that people took advantage of this and didn't pay Baba Dana her full pension entitlement at the local post office. She would talk and laugh so loudly, I sometimes thought she had a built-in loudspeaker somewhere. You could hear her coming from one end of the village to the other.

I'll always remember going to Serbia to collect her and bring her over just before my Mum died, and it was her 4th trip to London. It was November 1999, and because of the war in Yugoslavia, and the NATO bombings earlier that year, there were no flights into Belgrade, Serbia's capital city. So I had to fly to Budapest and travel on an overnight bus to cross the border. There was an eerie silence on the bus once we got to Serbia, and I got to see the effects of the bombs and missiles that had been dropped on the city. I saw tall buildings with massive missile shaped holes in them, and could feel the energy of a country that has been attacked – the desolateness that comes from the destructive energy of war. From the City, I got the coach to my grandmother's village.

The farmer across the road from my grandmother gave us a lift to the bus station when we were leaving. As we were driving in his 1950s style Yugo car, he started to laugh loudly, exclaiming "How is it that I went to school, studied hard, learnt to read and write, run my own farm.......and you, an illiterate old peasant farmhand is off abroad – no, to a big city like LONDON - for the 4th time?!?!?!". Baba Dana loved him – they were like an argumentative but loving brother and sister – and just sat in the car laughing and laughing and laughing. It was so funny and beautiful.

Her first visit to the UK was when I was 8 years old. She travelled back with us when we were returning from our summer holidays and it was amazing to see the experience through her eyes. I always felt like we were going back in time when we went to see her. Our Yugoslav friends would ask us what it was like to have tea with the Queen, or to see Michael Jackson, but for my Baba Dana coming over to the UK...well, it must have been like visiting the furthest reaches of outer space. For those that have seen the film Borat, her village was like his village, and the way he at first stumbles going down on the escalator when he arrives in the US is exactly what she did. She got herself stuck in the airplane toilet, because she couldn't work out how to push/pull the concertina doors....and she couldn't read the instructions. The helpful communist era "we're not paid to smile, just to throw food and orders at you" flight attendants just shouted at her for holding up the other passengers. The first time she had EVER seen a black person was then.....she blatantly put her hand out and pointed at this man, whilst tugging at my mum's sleeve, asking "how can he walk down the road like that?!".........My mum's reply was simple and no-nonsense: "In the very same way that you can".

Baba Dana was a bit embarrassing to us as kids. She would chase our friends away if she thought they were taking anything of ours (she interpreted any sharing as stealing), shouting and swearing in Serbian. We learnt very quickly to never look like we were looking for anything that we may have lost.......she once spent 2 days literally going through every square millimetre of her small 1 bedroom cottage because of something we'd mislaid.....and no amount of getting her to sit down counted. I guess my stubbornness comes from that Slavic school of tenacity; in fact there are different words for it in Serbian, depending on what *degree* of stubbornness you are talking about.

Anything involving pain or tragedy can be very uncomfortable for us reserved stiff upper lip Brits (relatively speaking, at least)......but my Baba Dana would wail and plead with God and shout "Kuku mene!" or "woe is me!" again and again over small things as well as big things. When I made the difficult decision to tell her that my Mum – her daughter – was dying, I decided to do so whilst on a walk outside of our house. I didn't want my Mum to hear the wailing I knew would follow, and knew I had to face. When I eventually told Baba Dana the truth about what was happening to my Mum, she just howled and wailed, begged and pleaded with God to take her arms, her legs, her heart, her eyes..... anything....*anything*.....so that her daughter could live, whilst beating her chest and pulling her hair with her large strong farmhand fists. I could see the neighbours' curtains twitching as we stood by the little park in our road, and felt more than a little embarrassed.

We didn't do manners. We slurped our tea. We would eat with our mouths open. We farted loudly. Actually, correction.....my brother, sister and I had limits. My mum used to fart loudly on purpose in public places, just to hear us go "Mum!!!" which used to make her laugh out loud.

My Mum was a really funny woman. A strict mother, but a wise, kind, and generous soul too. Actually, I would like to say that she was as mad as a box of frogs, in the best possible ways, and I guess now that she's on the "other side" I can freely. It was her eccentricity that made her brilliant.

Separately to her natural eccentricity, she had bipolar affective disorder, and every 4 years or so would have a full psychotic breakdown, when she believed there were bombs and firing squads everywhere. Even when she was having a breakdown – as hard work and intense as it was to see and be around – she also managed to be really funny at times too. She would remember what she did when she had got better, and bless her, even though she was embarrassed about it, would try with us at lease to laugh at some of the things she had done, which was how we would all heal a bit from the experience. She wouldn't sleep for a week or so, and would call friends at 3am with major life revelations, and make us all stay in the front room and not leave because of the firing squad outside the front room door, so I would have to stay awake and chaperone her at all times. She thought there were bombs everywhere.

My favourite thing that she would do would happen whenever we had to go out to see the psychiatrist. We didn't have a car, and not much money and taxis were a luxury so we had to walk the mile to get there. She believed every red car had a bomb in it, so when one drove down the road, she'd do some crazy-arsed James Bond style ninja move, pin me to the nearest wall or hedge shouting "if they're going to kill anyone, they will kill me first". The confusion on her face once the red car had passed, and no bomb had gone off, was actually very sweet to see.

When she was well, in addition to her natural eccentricity, she wouldn't understand normal western ways of living and behaving due to her peasant farming Slavic background. She would shout for "Durex" ("Doorex") really loudly in her heavy Serbian accent in shops when she meant "Duracell", would wear bling gold, and would breathe in front of my friends....you know, the stuff we worry about as teenagers. What made it worse for me in my teenage years was that she was – well – into *natural* stuff. Like organic food and natural toiletries, which was so *unfashionable* and *weird* back then.

It took me a while to realize that my mother was a trend-setting ultra cool genius with regards to natural health and organic food - some time after she had passed in fact, bless her wise heart. Oh how she laughs from the "other side".

At my brother's graduation, when we gathered in a courtyard with the other families, patiently waiting for our educated sons/daughters/siblings to leave the ceremony hall and find us, she stood on a raised platform next to a statue in the middle of the courtyard so she could see and be seen by all and shouted "Alex!!!" several times, in her thick heavy Slavic accent, very loudly.

To people in my community, having "Tea At The Ritz" was the epitome of luxury and wealth. Whenever I borrowed money from my mum as a student (only when really desperate), and promised to pay it back, she would joke "don't worry, you can take me for Tea At The Ritz with your first pay packet". I could always tell she didn't believe that she would ever experience something that luxurious; it was a little joke that could easily have been replaced with "Trip To The Moon", for how much of a possibility she thought it was. So for her 47th birthday, her last birthday before she passed, I arranged for us all to go in a Roll Royce – my Mum's favourite car – for Tea At The Ritz, with the help of my brother. It was a secret surprise, and her only instructions were that she was to dress beautifully.

On the morning of her birthday, we had an argument – I can't remember what about now – but for the first time, following years of destructive arguing, I learnt how to respond kindly, fairly and in a loving way with my Mum. Only now can I see how much she just wanted and needed parenting herself. My Mum, sensing she had "lost" this particular argument, said "oh! you don't love me – or you wouldn't argue with me......so I don't want your birthday present. And anyway, how can you argue with me....I've got cancer!". So I gently replied "of course I love you Mum, but that doesn't mean we won't disagree or argue. As for your cancer......as far as I am concerned, as long as you have a breath in your lungs, you are alive and responsible for yourself and your behaviour. We have arranged this birthday treat because we love you, and are all really excited about it, and want to take you, but it is completely up to you whether you go or not. You need to tell me soon, though, so I can cancel the arrangements if you don't want to come." She went very quiet, looked at her feet and said "OK, I will come".

The Rolls Royce driver was a wonderful man who knew that we wanted to keep the location a surprise until we arrived, so we got my Mum to guess where we were going. She listed all sorts of places, including The Ritz – which we laughed off, in the same way we laughed off everything else. "Tea at The Ritz? What do you think – that we're made of money?!" I laughed. When we pulled up in front of it, I happened to be sitting in the perfect place to see my Mum's reaction as she realised where we were, it was so beautiful. Her whole face lit up, her mouth wide open with joyous surprise, as though we had just taken a kid into a sweet shop, and told her she could have all of the sweets she wanted. It was one of the happiest expressions I ever saw her make, and still makes me cry now, remembering it. But she didn't leave her peasant farming roots at the door. Oh no. They came for Tea At The Ritz too.

I was really struck how you could tell the difference between the "genuinely rich" visitors and the tourists like us. The rich people dressed beautifully but very simply, and ate just enough from the "eat as much as you like" trays of sandwiches, scones and cakes. Us poor lot were dressed like we had gone to sit in the Royal Box at the theatre, and ate as much as we possibly could stuff our faces with, like we were at an "all you can eat buffet". My Mum was in heaven. Or her heaven. And it was so wonderful to see that the staff – especially our waiter – treated us no differently to anyone else. He was equally as lovely and charming, but had an extra twinkle in his eye for us – like he could tell how much it meant to us all. We polished off three lots of sandwiches. It was the first time we had eaten sandwiches with the crusts cut off.

When the cakes came out, they were decorated with perfect little chocolate plaques on them, saying "The Ritz". I was amazed to see the waiter be so beautifully polite and obliging to my Mum, who had a plan for the little chocolate plaques. She sat up, all pleased with herself, with an "Aha!". She told us she had had an idea. This was never a good sign. She told us that she was going to remove all the plaques, take them home, put them on her own cakes and make out they were from The Ritz. Our pleas of "Mum, what are you doing? Oh My God, you are so embarrassing" as she beckoned the waiter over didn't stop her....and she asked him for big piece of foil from the kitchen. He was so wonderful, and just obliged. We have a wonderful photo of her proudly standing in the lobby on the way out, with her little bundle of foil containing the wrapped chocolate Ritz plaques.

The other thing that struck me was how, when the pianist played happy birthday and an extra cake with a candle was brought out for my Mum, everyone – rich and poor – applauded my Mum like she was the Queen. It was so beautiful – I really felt the generosity of spirit of everyone who genuinely meant their applause. In that moment, of celebrating the life of a person - money did not separate anyone in any way. My Mum had a lovely chat with the pianist afterwards, who asked her what her favourite song was and then played her a song from the musical Phantom of the Opera, which she adored. She talked about her birthday treat of Tea At The Ritz to anyone who would listen for the remaining 6 months of her life.

Her love of her peasant farming manners would follow her to the most amazing times and places. A few weeks after we had been for Tea At The Ritz, she had a moment of total brilliance in hospital. She sat in her hospital bed, slurping her tea like a proper Serbian peasant *totally on purpose* to see which of the ladies sitting opposite her would start to struggle with "the bloody foreigner" as my mum used to call herself. The fact that we had just been told that her lung cancer had spread to her brain, and that her cancer was now terminal, wasn't going to get in the way of my mum's sense of fun. She wanted to cheer me up between the bouts of me running to the loo to cry, trying to hide my tears and sorrow out of sight of my dying Mama. Watching the other patients twitching behind their newspapers as my Mum slurped her tea on purpose was hilarious. We giggled like children. The enormity of her strength, her courage and her sense of fun were captivating.

My Mum was the one patient that the chemo nurses loved seeing the most when I would take her for her chemo sessions. I would look around and see patients and families looking so miserable, depressed, sad and grey. Not my Mum. She used it as an opportunity to make me, and herself and the nurses laugh and laugh. It used to piss the other patients and their families off for rudely interrupting their misery; the glares that would be sent in our direction at times astounded me. My Mum didn't want me to be sad. She wasn't going to let anything get in the way of making the best of what was happening in any way she could. I know she was doing that for me more than for herself.

She didn't shed a tear the day we knew her cancer was terminal, or the 6 months that followed before her passing, or indeed any of the last year since her first diagnosis. Maybe it was the mood stabilising drugs, but I think she knew it was her time. I also feel she was tired of this life and wanted some peace. And actually, it just wasn't her style. In fact she would laugh at how she had had to console a male friend of hers who sobbed loudly on her shoulder when he found out about her cancer. In public. In front of the neighbours. She didn't know what to do other than gently pat him on his back, saying "there, there, it's OK" whilst hoping this embarrassing moment would stop immediately.

This was the measure of my Mum, strong and funny, she just did her own thing. I think I was born feisty because she was. She was 47 years old when she died. Even though she was bright and brilliant, and funny and strong, she was already tired too.

8

There were many reasons why my Mum was tired of her life.

My mother's father ("Deda") was a steam engine driver and a published poet. My Mum didn't talk about him much – I don't think she ever truly allowed herself to grieve for him, but she told me some things. He used to take her in the engine of the steam train with him sometimes. He was away from home a lot, but when he was there, he adored my mum. Apparently, he wasn't loving to Baba Dana or my aunt, but there was something about my mum that he truly cherished. I think it was her spark....her cheekiness. When she was naughty (which apparently was all the time), he would go the local ice-cream maker where he had a tab, and tell them that she wasn't allowed anymore ice-creams. So she would wait a couple of days before going in and telling them that he had said it was fine to give her ice-creams again now. He bought her her favourite winter coat. But he had a darker side; and had behaved in ways that were quite common at the time culturally. He had, apparently, raped my Baba Dana, and so she was considered to be unmarriable as she was no longer a virgin. So Baba Dana then followed him around for the rest of his life, because she would not have been able to be with any other man. They never married, which was unheard of; he never made "an honest woman" out of her. But somehow, she was accepted in her community. They were, thankfully, able to see past her "unmarried mother" status and love her. His behaviour with Baba Dana did not get in the way of him really loving my mum, however. I have always been intrigued by that. I guess that even those we judge in society as being "horrible" or "dangerous" or "violent" have a place where their heart is free and loving.

Deda had a stroke and died when my mum was just 10 years old. As her mother worked in the fields all day just to buy bread, there was no one to look after Mum after school. A "kindly" offer of help came from a man in the village who offered to look after my mum after school. He raped her from when she was 11 to when she was 16. When she turned 16, and couldn't cope anymore, she ran away from home to the nearest town. She arrived there, was scared about what to do next, and so went to the police station and asked for help. In those days, there was a strongly held belief that it was always the "woman's fault"; even if a small child; that she "asked for it" or "tempted the man". So the police took her home, and when the villagers gathered around the car to see what was going on, the police told everyone what my mother had said. The following day, her abuser threw himself under a train. My mother was blamed for his death. In fact, the whole village ostracised her for the two years she remained there, with only her mother, sister and two friends speaking to her.

Once I had understood what had happened to her, seeing how those same villagers behaved towards her when we would visit was really distressing to me. My Mum would go into a lot of debt to buy suitcases full of the products that communist-era Yugoslavians couldn't easily get hold of – razor blades, nylon tights, bags and bags of coffee, medicines and even lipsticks and hairdyes too. The villagers would queue up to come and see what my Mum had brought them. Once I knew her story, I I saw them as vultures, it made me so angry that the last time I went back (until I went to collect my grandmother) was when I was 15 years old. That, and the fact that I had been sexually assaulted, and no amount of my Mum pleading with the JAT (Yugoslav) Airline office to change our flights home meant anything. Nothing had changed in the intervening years since my mother's childhood – the assault was definitely in the eyes of the JAT staff My Fault.

My mother never told me the full story of what happened to her as child herself. Once, on a bus to Selfridges in London, we sat on the top deck so she could smoke (back in the days when we could smoke on public transport!?!). She half told me the story, but told me she had just been beaten. She never told me about the man's death or how she had been ostracised. I was 11 at the time. I remember sitting next to mum, trying to hide the vast and overwhelming tears of sadness that were pouring down my face for her, because I could feel and see what had really happened to her using my intuition, although I didn't know I had it at the time. I saw the sexual abuse; I could see part of her journey. I had this confirmed and found out the rest of the story through that time honoured tradition of a growing child's life - earwigging on a conversation she had with a friend.

My mum loved Selfridges. It was a haven to her – I think it was because she had known such poverty that to her it was an oasis of beauty, abundance, possibility, glitz and glamour. We were forever struggling with money, but when she did buy something, it would be of a high quality, pricey and preferably from Selfridges. I reckon their shares dipped a bit after she died. No £40 plastic liquidiser for us. No....it had to be the designer £150 version (1998 prices). No £40 smoothie maker.......it had to be the designer £250 centrifugal force juice extractor (again 1999 prices). Before anyone else know what juicers were.

When she eventually renovated the kitchen (I think we actually were the last family in Britain to get a fitted kitchen, like we were the last family to get a VHS video player – at least we waited long enough to know the outcome of the VHS/BetaMax debate), she got an all-singing and all-dancing 6-ring 2-oven cooker. When she saw on the telly that the Duchess of York (Fergie) had the very same one in her kitchen too, she would then tell everyone who would hear her, in her strong Serbian accent "Ah ha!!! Seeee.......if eet eez gud eenuf forrr Ferrrrgie, eet eeez gud eenuf forr meee". When she got a Selfridges storecard despite having no money (!) I asked my little sister why she didn't intervene when my mum rushed around the kitchen department taking one of everything in sight. "You know how she is" my then 11 year old sister replied "she got that glint in her eye....there was nothing anyone could have done". Her best friend and me argued with her for three weeks about the amazing sheepskin coat that she had put a deposit down on. It was £2800....well £3000 "eeef yu inclood de haat, vich eez a barrrrgin aat £200"). We thought that the fact that she was dying with cancer and would probably only ever wear it once, and we had no idea how we would pay for her funeral or debts as it was, was a reasonable argument at the time. If only I knew then what I know now, I would have so gone with her and supported her enjoying every moment of that precious joy to her, despite my disagreement with the use of fur. The day she died, we inherited a bunch of debts but probably the most well-equipped kitchen in London.

My mum only ever told my father and 2 friends the story of her abuse. My father's obsession with my virginity, telling my brother to only ever marry a virgin, knowing that my mother hadn't had that choice, was a very harsh thing he would say in front of my Mum.

Many years later, I asked for my mum to be admitted to a psychiatric hospital because her frustration and explosions during her 4th breakdown were too much for my then 6 year old sister to cope with, who had got scared. I asked a psychiatrist why they were only discharging her with yet more medication. I wanted to know why she wasn't having any therapy. In fact, to my knowledge, she had never had any therapy. My mum was present and went very quiet as I started to – angrily – ask the psychiatrist whether they had on their files any notes on her childhood. On why, during her breakdowns, she would be terrified that she or we were being persecuted or in danger or were about to be killed. I asked the psychiatrist if they had records of my mother's abuse, of whether anyone had ever tried to understand her "madness", which to me was perfectly understandable given her experiences? The psychiatrist looked sheepish as she apologetically admitted that they didn't have any of this recorded in her notes. I felt guilty for a long time for having revealed something so profoundly personal to my mother in a way that I know reminded her of the shame she sadly felt. Even though we never spoke about it afterwards, and I know she felt really embarrassed, I really felt that some part of her felt an almost childlike happiness and relief that someone was finally speaking up and saying it was unacceptable that she had experienced all she had. I felt she knew I was trying, in my own clumsy 17-year old way to stand up for her; to try to help her. It was one of the very few times in her life that anyone ever did defend her, rather than her having to do it for herself, as her name had called her to do.

9

Not only was I different – my family were always different. We didn't fit in, as a family. Not with the Serbian community, not in the UK. Even though we lived in the UK, there was a definite hierarchy in the Serbian community. Actually, it felt like the caste system to be honest at times. There is the equivalent of the Women's Institute (WI) – it is called "The Circle of Serbian Women". They raise money, bake cakes, sew costumes for the folk dancing group; that kind of thing. Now it is run by a wonderful friend of mine, and a new generation is bringing a new energy that is inclusive and brilliant and loving.

But when I was growing up, there was the "in crowd" and the "out crowd". We weren't political, or into sucking up to anyone, and basically came from an unglamorous peasant background. Well actually, most of the community did, but lots of people denied this I think. We were definitely in the "out crowd". My father was a difficult man. My Mum didn't wear make up or posh clothes. She had huge amounts of integrity. My Mum was part of the Circle, and tended to be given the jobs no-one else wanted to do. She never complained, she always did them lovingly. There is a photo of her standing on the altar steps in the church, with all of the women in the Circle there together, but she is standing on the edge, slightly separated from the group. She is beaming and proud. It was as though everyone knew she didn't quite fit in, including her, but that she loved what she did, so she didn't let that stop her. That was my Mum "to a "T"".

Even though my upbringing was Christian Orthodox, there is a strong undercurrent of mystery and magic in the Serbian culture, and no amount of frowning on this by the church has ever truly diminished it. My mother was a true teacher of being in one's own strength and power. She taught me how to interpret dreams according to the traditions of her elders. She would read coffee cups for friends (which is a bit like reading tea leaves), but always told people that she wasn't any good. Even though she could not tell anyone in her community about this, she would talk to me about the stars and say "no-one can tell me that, with all those millions of stars in the sky, that this is the only planet in this Universe with life on it". She tried to read an English version of the Qu'ran, because she felt that it was important to understand other people's religions and not judge – which given her upbringing and community influences and the era this was happening, was groundbreaking. Only her lack of strong English made it impossible to finish the English translation.

She was a bit of rule breaker – she always did things her way. She lived by 2 mottos. The first one was "ne daj se" which means "don't surrender (who you are)". I think that's the call to those of us who are feisty. The second, knowing that people called her "Luda Branka" ("Mad Branka") for the choices she would make, like getting us scholarships for private schools, or growing organic food, or buying natural toiletries was to say "Neka, neka, pusti ih, vidiće" ("Let them [talk], let them [talk], they'll see"). She always did things her way – the way that felt intuitively right to her – no matter what anyone thought. I really now believe that we choose the key people in our lives before we are born, as so beautifully described in Michael Newton's *Life Between Lives,* and I think that's partly why I chose her to be my Mum.

There were three things she loved most in the world. Firstly, and always the most, us. Her children. She literally did live for us. She missed her homeland in the most heartaching ways, but refused to move back because she would then be without us.

Then she loved her garden. She had a vegetable patch at the back where she grew amazing tomatoes, and cabbages, cauliflowers, onions and potatoes. She planted as many fruit trees as she could – we had a cherry tree, plum tree, apple trees, a pear tree, an apricot tree and a nectarine tree. She was happy in the garden and would talk to all the trees and plants she grew, proud of how they flourished with her love and care. Her favourite flowers were roses, and she collected many varieties. I say "collected" but what I actually mean is *stole.* She had absolutely no qualms about taking clippings of roses she loved from other people's gardens. "Shhhhhhh!" she'd quickly say if we would protest what she was doing to a rose bush we'd stopped to admire. She didn't want us to draw attention to her thievery. What was amazing to witness was how Mum's garden died with her when she passed. Literally nothing grew back. She loved her flowers and plants and veggies and trees, and they loved her. They didn't want to be without her tender loving care.

And finally she loved Molly, our pure white pedigree cat. My Mum had had a dream once, that she won the jackpot on the Pools (the equivalent of the lottery back then). She dreamed of becoming, as her cheque book holder said, and she would laugh about in her strong Serbian accent, a "rich bitch!". In the dream was this pure white cat. So my Mum decided that we needed a pure white cat. Let me remind you of something. My Mum was a peasant farming Slav. Peasant farming Slavs do not buy pedigree animals, especially not *pets*. This was a little ridiculous. What made it all the more ridiculous was that we had no money. Despite this, my Mum borrowed £400 back then (worth about £1200 now) to buy Molly. All because of a dream she'd had. And ADORED her. They had a lovely relationship. I will always remember the sadness I could feel in my Mum, 6 months before she herself died, when we had to put 17 year old Molly to sleep. She never did win the Pools, or the lottery. But she loved Molly.

Even though she wasn't part of the "in" crowd, and nor were we as a family, I will always remember and be grateful for how packed our church was at her funeral. It was beautiful to see. So many people, people I knew, and people I didn't, told me what a wonderful, wonderful woman she was, kind and generous and giving and loving. We laughed a lot at how funny she could be.

I loved going to our church. I still do, even though I am not religious anymore. The smell of incense, the choir singing the Eastern version of Gregorian chanting throughout each service, that quiet, peaceful devotion to prayer, stillness and God. Orthodox church services really are beautiful.

In Serbian and Russian Orthodox churches (but not in Greek churches), you have to stand throughout the service. Chairs are provided around the edge of the church for those who are old, frail or pregnant. There is such a stigma about sitting on them that basically, people avoid using them unless they are actually about to fall into a coma. But you don't have to be there for the whole service, you can just pop in for a bit and then leave when your legs start to hurt. Perfect for pseudo-Christians and teenagers.

My father used to take me when I was very small. I have memories from when I was maybe 4 years old. I used to stand so still, because I wanted him to think that I was good. I was so still in fact, that I probably looked like a waxwork. Because I couldn't understand the big words used in the service, I used to follow his cues for when to draw a cross across myself during key times of prayer. The moment I would sense, out of the corner of my eye, that he was about to move his hand, I would get ready to move mine too. I would make sure we moved our hands at exactly the same time. Except sometimes he then would go to scratch his head instead. So, not knowing what to do with my hands, I would copy him. I was behaving a bit like a mini-me, I suppose.

I would hear the words of the priest singing about the joys of heaven and the punishments for those destined to go to hell, and I would be having a chat with God. Apart from the fact that he looked like a friendly, grandfatherly, white-bearded man, he was nothing like this old testament portrayal to me. My God was (is) kind, loving. We used to joke around a bit while I talked to him, in my head, during the church services. He used to tease me in a loving fatherly way – the way I wish my own father had done with me. He made me feel safe. And so very, very loved. And free. Like I could do anything and it would be OK – because he loved me. So I used to *love* going to church – because I would have these experiences that definitely broke the rules, and were beautiful.

I was 7 years old when I first saw an angel. She was soooooo beautiful, I felt completely at peace, while she beamed at me one night. I remember going back to sleep, having a rare moment when I was young of feeling completely safe and happy. I was shortly before I saw the angel that saved my Mama from the concrete paving slab my father threw.

I guess that angels have always kept me safe.

I first ran away from home when I was 8 years old, and I think I most definitely had angels helping me then.

My parents had bought me a very expensive 22 carat gold crucifix and matching chain, which had my name engraved on it and had been blessed by the priest. They told me I had to wear it All The Time. When I explained that I wasn't allowed to wear jewellery at school, my mother suggested I hide it under my tops, and no one would know. I got the message. I Had To Wear It No Matter What.

We were still young enough to do gym classes at school in the school hall in our vests and knickers (or pants). When I was getting ready for gym one day, I realised that I might get into trouble for wearing a necklace, so I carefully took it off and tucked it away in a corner of the hall, hoping it would stay safe until the end of the class. Someone else must have seen it, though, and taken it. I couldn't tell a teacher because I should not have been wearing it in the first place, so I just kept quiet and didn't tell anyone. I hoped my parents wouldn't notice. But of course my Mum did one evening.

My Mum gave me a beating so hard that evening that I was covered in bruises, all over my arms and legs and body. I remember feeling quite numb after a while – I blocked the experience emotionally, and just "took it". I did, however, decide that I couldn't live at home anymore and would run away.

The next day, I told my friend Claire, and asked if I could run away to her house and live with her. Of course she said yes, and that her Mum Would Completely Understand, and we could live together and be like sisters.

So that evening, as soon as my mother took my brother to his Karate class, leaving me home alone, I packed my orange swimming bag with lots of pairs of pants and socks. I left with a carefully drawn map of how to walk the 2km to her house, which involved crossing Horn Lane - a crazy road akin to something you would find in India back then, with no distinct lanes, and drivers weaving in and out on either side of each other. I remember taking a deep breath, and asking God to look after me as I stepped onto Horn Lane, and breathing a sigh of relief once I had got to the other side.

Claire's mother was very surprised to see me. Claire's explanation of our plan didn't help her to see that I should come and live with them instead. She was so very lovely though. I sat in Claire's room, on Claire's bed, next to Claire, talking to her mum. I showed her some of my bruises, not realising what might then happen. She persuaded me to let her phone my Mum and tell her I was OK, and then eventually persuaded me to let my Mum pick me up and take me home. I felt very embarrassed about it all, and was upset I might have worried my Mum. I remember feeling really very uncomfortable as my Mum hugged me tightly when we got home, and wouldn't let me go, sobbing over me, and apologising for what had happened.

I knew my Mum didn't mean it. I knew my Mum wasn't violent in her core. I knew she adored me. I knew she had snapped – that things were just too much for her, and I just happened to be there when it happened. So I knew things were escalating in a way I didn't want when I saw Claire's Mum talking to my form teacher, Ms Hussey, the following morning at the start of school. I felt really apprehensive when Ms Hussey told me that there would be some people coming in to talk to me about what had happened to me at home. I was taken out of a lesson later that morning and to a quiet room at the other end of the school. I had never been taken out of a lesson before. I was told that there were some people there called Social Workers, who were there to help me and my Mum. They told me I wasn't going to get into trouble, and that my Mum wasn't going to get into any trouble either. They persuaded me to eventually show them my bruises. I hated doing it, I was angry that I felt I had to show them – I knew it would get my Mum into trouble, despite what they said, but I didn't know how to tell them that it wasn't my Mum's fault. That it was my father who was the problem. Because I didn't have the language, and confidence, and understanding to explain to them that my Mum was a good person, a kind person, who wasn't coping, I just spent the whole meeting feeling ashamed and exposed and vulnerable, helpless and angry.

I always thought it was ironic that we were placed on the "At Risk Register" with Social Services because of the actions of my Mum. She wasn't a bad person, she just had a lot of problems, and actually was quite ill, but she really loved us and I felt it. She just had – as Michael Douglas's film captured – a "Falling Down" moment. If we were to be on the register, I always thought it should've been because of my father. I don't think my mother ever got over us being on the register because of her – she was then terrified for the many years we remained on it, that we would be taken away from her because the State had deemed her an unfit mother.

Shortly after this, she had her first full psychotic breakdown, and was sectioned.

I have always struggled with the smacking debate based on my experiences. I personally don't believe that hitting children is the answer. However, to criminalise parents who are loving, but who may not be coping, is not helpful, I feel. I believe it then puts those usually loving parents in the same category as people like my father, who are wilfully violent and abusive with their children. Even as a child, I knew the difference between the "not coping" beating from my mother who adored me but had fallen apart and the destructive abusive violence from my father. They were worlds apart. I think it makes loving parents feel terrible about having moments of being pushed to the limit, and doesn't separate them from those abusers who cause real harm. Also, I think it makes it hard for loving parents who are struggling to cope to ask for help. Being a parent is hard at the best of times – I would love a world where we were better able to support people who are finding it hard to cope free from judgement, with more open arms of love and kindness.

The next time I ran away from home, I was 14 years old. Ironically it was – again – because of a situation with my Mum. I can't remember what had happened. My mother – out of fear of me experiencing the same abuse that she had done as a child – did everything she could to stop me going out and spending time with my friends. I couldn't go to sleepovers, or to parties, have boyfriends – all the things my friends could do. So I was expected to be at home every evening living in a miserable and dangerously unpredictable family situation, with the threat of extreme violence or death at any time, but I couldn't go out, escape it all and have fun. So we started to argue. I was angry with my Mum for a) bringing me into this life and b) stopping me from living a life away from the pain (as I saw it). She would go through my belongings to check what I was up to. She would read my letters, there was nowhere that was safe for me to just be me.

I wish I had known back then what I only relatively recently came to understand. She was only barely holding it together between hospital breakdowns. She was terrified about me dying, or something awful happening to me, like happened to her. She was also hugely dependent on me emotionally, and couldn't cope with me growing up and away from her. I think she was in part also intuiting my future, and was doing everything she could, in her way, to try to keep me safe from her deepest fears by keeping me at home.

But I didn't understand my Mum back then, and I most certainly didn't understand the hell my life felt that it was. So I went wild. Like a caged animal desperate to escape I did everything I could to stay away from what felt to me a prison of pain being home.

The first time I ran away in my teen years, I phoned a schoolfriend from a payphone, and told her that I was running away. She asked me what my plans were, and I think I told her I was going to sleep in the park. She told me to stop being silly – that if I could time arriving in front of her house at an exact set time, that she would sneak downstairs with her Mum's keys, and get me into the garage. It felt like we were arranging some kind of secret mission – it felt exciting, and dangerous (what if we got caught?), and......freeing. I realised I was out, alone, on my own, doing my thing. Breathing in that night air felt amazing – and addictive. It was like a jack in a box had popped out – and would never be squeezed in again.

So I showed up at my friend's house at the exact time, feeling very nervous in case her parents heard her unlock her front door, or caught us in any way. She managed to sneak out, unnoticed and snuck me into their garage. I slept on bits of old cut up carpet on the concrete floor that night. It was uncomfortable – have I mentioned my big hips (?!) – but the freedom I felt was far beyond any discomfort. Until I needed to go for a wee at about 6am.

My friend crept in to give me a few mouthfuls of her porridge and to sneak me into the loo when her parents weren't watching at about 7.30am. I had been BURSTING to pee for over an hour and a half. I did everything I could to hold it in, but I did get a little bit of leakage. The thing was, I was in my uniform, and had no access to clean clothes or a shower. I knew I would have to go to my posh private school that day unwashed, and smelling a bit of wee. Which was a bit embarrassing, so I spent the whole day trying to sit with my legs crossed or a mile from anyone I was talking to, so they couldn't smell me too closely.

Our Deputy Headmistress, Ms Ross, came to one of our classes that morning, and asked to see me. She took me to her office, where a police officer wanted to know where I had been, as my mother had reported me missing to the police. I lied. I think I might have been a bit stroppy with him. I was starting to develop an attitude.

It became a bit of a regular occurrence. In fact, for a whole year, my posh private school that I attended thanks to a Government scholarship scheme, became used to the regular visits from the police when I had been – yet again – reported missing by my Mum. At one point it was a weekly event.

My teachers and the school were fantastic about it – I am sure they had never seen anything like it before; there really never was any trouble at our school – but I think they valued that I always showed up. The thing is, it didn't matter where I slept – usually with friends, but a couple of times on the streets as well – I would always, ALWAYS go to school. I was on time, in my uniform. Sometimes I didn't have the right books or equipment, but I was always there, ready to learn, to see my friends, to be in my place of safety. There was only one occasion when a teacher got angry with me for not having the right books with me......and he was a wonderful, inspirational, funny teacher that we all adored, so my guess is he was having a bad day. It was the first lesson after I last slept on the streets, and the week I went into foster care, and I think the teachers were told later that day what was happening for me. For the month after that, he was super lovely to me. I think it was his way for saying sorry for shouting at me.

The first time I slept on the streets, I was 15. I had asked so many friends to stay at theirs, that I didn't feel able to ask yet again. I phoned my then boyfriend, but he was out. Well, I wasn't going home. So that meant I had to find somewhere safe to sleep under the stars. It was a school night – it must have been, because I slept in my school uniform. I knew that made me extra vulnerable – that I was at risk of attracting pimps, dealers and worse. Out of uniform, I looked much older than my years, but uniformed......well, uniforms only get worn by schoolgirls. This was in the days before "school disco" nights out.

I went to my ex's flat in Gospel Oak, just in case he had returned home. His Mum, who ran a stall at Camden market, told me he was out. So I walked the streets around Gospel Oak and then Hampstead Heath for what felt like hours, trying to kill time. Eventually I came across a very wealthy road in Hampstead, with huge 5 and 6 bedroomed family homes. It felt like a very safe place. One house had a garage that had a short driveway that went steeply down under the house – and there was a small area in front of the garage doors that was under the house. It looked like a perfect place in the shadows, out of the way of prying eyes, with shelter. I sat upright, against the garage door, with my knees tucked under my chin. I was cold, and for the first time ever I felt completely alone, totally abandoned by my parents, by my life, by God. Then it started to rain. Even though it was dry in my place in the shadows, it was like the skies were releasing the tears I needed to let flow. But I felt I couldn't cry; that I would just need to keep going, staying strong, facing the world and my life alone.

I didn't acknowledge this at the time, but in later years, when I would think about which moment in time was the point in which I felt most abandoned by God, the angels, by Life itself, this was it. I don't think I can convey what it feels like to sleep on the streets, even for a night. It felt like I had become nothing, invisible, like there was no place in the world for me to exist and to be and to be safe. I felt completely disconnected from ordinary people who had safe warm comfortable homes, and beds and lives, I couldn't understand how their lives were like that. Still to this day, I have to fight back tears when I see homeless people, the pain I feel at seeing where they are cuts me to my core.

I cry easily. At everything. I feel people's pain. I feel people's joy. I feel helpless sometimes looking at this beautiful world and the ways humankind can behave towards one another upsets me so much I can't speak but my red streaming eyes show the pain and sorrow my heart does feel. Seeing homeless people does this to me. My heart literally hurts.

I would be more willing one day to go and volunteer in a war zone using my skills, than to a homeless shelter at Christmas, which sounds crazy perhaps, but it's still too raw for me even now. I give money freely, and pray and ask for healing and help for the people I meet on the streets, and when I don't have any cash to give, I try to always look at a homeless person in the eyes and say "I'm so sorry, but I just don't have any cash", but I can never spend too much time talking to homeless people, even so many years and a ton of healing and therapy later, because it still upsets me to my core. It's just so wrong in our abundant world that we have so many empty properties and yet so many people are without a place to sleep and have nowhere to go when they are desperate. It's one of the first changes I would make if I was a political leader.

I was desperate and I continued to run away, with another experience of sleeping on the streets before I finally asked Social Services – at the age of 16 – to place me into care.

It was late on a Saturday night when I slept on the top floor of a block of flats. It seemed a safe place, with a buzzer system on the main entrance, so I knew I wouldn't be bothered by random people. I don't know how I had learned this by that age in my life – I had never been in a block of flats with a buzzer system that I remember, but I obviously knew that if I pressed the "Trade" buzzer, I might get myself in through the main entrance. It worked. I slept on the hard floor outside a flat with a beautiful cross on the door. It was simple, I think it was made by woven straw......but there was something very lovely, warm, homely and safe about it for me. I left at dawn in case someone found me. I hung around before going to my ex's in the afternoon. His Mum reluctantly let me stay the night, and I made sure I had made it to school by 8.30am on the Monday morning, travelling by tube to school. I had never seen rush hour on the Underground before. It was a revelation. And I knew my life was about to be different in more ways than how I would be travelling to school.

As soon as I arrived at school, I went to talk to my form teacher, Mrs Ranaraja – a wonderful French teacher. She always had that French "stern" look about her – as though it was sometimes difficult for her to smile - and was a bit scary before you got to know her. I suppose it helps discipline in a classroom if you have that air of being a bit scary, but she was lovely. I didn't know her very well, she had never taught me, and was only just my new form tutor. I explained that I couldn't go home anymore, and asked if I could possibly attend lessons flexibly that week, just so I could to sort out a new home. She was amazing. I had only just started the year – the first year of my A-Levels in fact, so any time missed was an issue, but she understood. She asked me to wait outside the staff room, before coming back a few minutes later with a key which she wanted to give to me. "You can't sleep on friend's floors. Come and stay at mine. I won't ever ask you where you are going, or what you are doing, but if you will be in at dinner time, let me know so I can make sure there is enough for you too". As I write this, I am crying at how beautiful and supported I felt in that moment.

I really resisted, in fact I didn't take the key. I didn't want to be a bother to anyone, but I let her know how grateful I was for her generosity and her understanding.

Then I went to the one and only pay phone in the school, outside the main changing rooms and toilets, and phoned Social Services, and asked to speak to a social worker. After explaining my situation, and asking to be placed into care, the social worker told me that – as I was 16 years old – I would need to contact the Homeless Persons Unit and access adult services. So, in my now well developed streetwise and at times argumentative feisty attitude, I basically told the social worker what her job was. Which was – given that I was still at school full-time - to find me a place to live, because if I contacted the Homeless Persons Unit, they would place me in a temporary B&B, and I would be surrounded by dodgy people like drug dealers and prostitutes, and then I wouldn't be able to study, and I would fail my A-Levels and my education, and how would she feel about that, when it was the duty of Social Services to house me?! I heard the resigned sigh in her voice as she made an appointment for me to be assessed later that day.

Before going to my appointment, the Deputy Headmistress at my school, Ms Ross, asked to see me. She asked me to reconsider Mrs Ranaraja's generous offer of somewhere to stay. I explained that I felt I couldn't accept it. She then said the following to me; something that has stayed with me my whole life: "Imagine if you had a home, and room in it. And someone you knew was in trouble, you would want to help them, wouldn't you?". I nodded enthusiastically. "And you would feel great being able to help someone, I would guess?", she continued. "Yes", I replied. "Well, Mrs Ranaraja has the ability to help you. You will help her to feel good about being able to help you, if you just say yes to staying at hers.".

I accepted Mrs Ranaraja's generous offer. As I left Ms Ross' office, she pointed out that I am just like my mother, which she said was a compliment, but it didn't feel like it at the time. I think she was referring to my Mum's tenacity and stubbornness.

At the assessment, I saw a wonderful Social Worker called Christine. That was on a Monday, and I was placed with my foster family on that Thursday. In the meantime, for the first time ever, I was woken every morning to a warm cup of tea, and toast with jam, and Mrs Ranaraja cared for me like she did her own daughter. She made a point of sitting with me one evening, after dinner, and just listening to me talking about my life. No-one had ever done that in that way before. She just listened, and she allowed me to feel heard by a responsible grown-up for the first time ever. Like it was going to be alright.

Joy, Rob and their 3 kids who were 1,2 and 3 at the time I started to live with them, lived a long way away. That was the first thing I thought when we travelled in the taxi to their home. It would later take me 90 minutes and 2 buses and a train to get to school each way every day, which felt like an age.

As Joy opened the door, and Christine introduced me as Danica, she said "oh we won't be able to remember that name, let alone pronounce it! Have you got a nickname at all?". I said sometimes people called me "Dennis" (a name one friend gave me when I was 10, after Dennis the Menace). She said "no, that's my sister's nickname - what about Dee?" I said "OK". And that was how Dee came about. When I finally returned to using Danica, some 20 years later, it took some friends 3 years to get around how to say my full name.

Usually people think about foster care as being a terrible experience. My experience was really positive. My foster family were – are - a lovely family. It was a tough year emotionally though. I still saw my Mum who was falling apart. She tried to kill herself during that year I was in foster care. Eventually, after I had spent a year in care, and when she had accepted that I needed to live my life my way, we found a way to become friends and I moved home ready for my final year at school.

My Mum was a wonderful wise soul, who had had a tough life, and I know I was a part of her life being hard. But despite the tough times, and despite the fact that she was really strict with me at times (she had no helpful parenting model), she was truly kind and big hearted. She would help anyone and everyone when they needed help, despite how broken her own life had been.

I remember the long conversations we had at one point when my father's second wife had phoned my Mum, asking my Mum for help. We had heard through the Serbian community grapevine that he had severely beaten his wife, so badly that she had been unable to leave her bed for 6 weeks. He had deliberately found a wife from his village in Serbia, and brought her over, someone he could control. She couldn't speak English and he forbade her from working or making friends. She was in many ways a prisoner. But she found my mother's number, and told her, on the phone, that she wanted to leave my father, and asked my Mum for help. It is a measure of the incredible compassion and generosity my Mum had that she agonised over what to do. She knew that she would be putting all of our lives at risk if she stepped in to help, but also knew that she couldn't leave this woman and their child to the mercy of my father. In the end, my Mum said that, if his wife could get to London from their Telford home, that my Mum would put them up for 3 days and nights – long enough to get help from the police and social services – but that 3 days and nights was the most she could do, on one promise. That my father was not to know. My Mum prepared to sleep on the sofa so his wife and daughter could have her bed. In the end, his wife never left him, but that my Mum was willing to do this was incredible to me.

When my friends stayed over once from University, she slept on the floor so we could all have a bed to sleep on.

That was the greatness of my Mum. Something I wish I had understood better as a teen. She was a really good person. Funny and wise and brilliant and loving. What I got to see was how broken she was too.

I am glad we made friends again before I headed to the bright lights and crazy fun of University life in Manchester. A city that felt like my true home, of such happiness and freedom and fun for the most part, that it would eventually become my chosen place to go home to die, in the same way that salmon do.

11

It was raving that saved me. As well as the angels, from heaven and on Earth, and my friends, of course. But raving, and music and dancing saved my life. Whoever said "God is a DJ" was right. Well I think so, anyway. My God is a DJ, with fuck off massive bass speakers the size of doors, and a love of Old Skool. And some fucking awesome decks.

It was my friend Marilyn, who I worked with on Saturdays in a chemist who first introduced me to raving. I was 15 years old, and went to see 808 State play Brixton Academy, one of my favourite venues in London, with N-Joi supporting. We were right at the front, and my eyes and mind and heart and soul exploded into life that night, seeing and feeling the magic of the music, and the dancing, and this culture of love. After the gig finished, a rave carried us through to 6am. This was it. I had found my place in the world, my piece of heaven on Earth. It was magic.

I was blown away by all the excitement, the number of people pouring out of Brixton tube station, all dressed up, made up, there was an amazing joyous buzz in the air unlike anything I had ever felt. Everything was new; queueing for ages in the cold to get in, talking to strangers who were really friendly, girls looking good in trainers, being searched to get in, and the thing that struck me the most was the noise. The noise levels – just of the excitement of people entering this old theatre that has been converted to a music venue – was amazing.

My love of dancing and music – especially deep soul-calling drum beats, and shrill cries of joy - began with Serbian folk dancing. It is a bit like a cross between Russian Kossack dancing and Greek circle dancing. The circle (or "kolo") is said to represent the neverending circle of life. At igranke (dances), people of all ages dance next to each other, from grandmothers to fathers holding their babies in their arms as they dance – and all are welcome into the circle for they are a part of it.

Classes run at the Serbian Community Centre, which children can start attending when they are 7 years old. Most of the kids have to be forced to go, complaining to their parents every week that "normal kids don't have to do it". There are always fewer boys than girls, so some of us girls learned the boys' dances as well as the girls. I have always been one of the few kids that loved it; it is fast, light on the feet with great fancy footwork. It has a life-affirming, powerful, uplifting energy to it. Even now when I hear the music, I can't sit still; I feel my heart explode with joy and passion and something much greater than me. It goes to the core of my being – as though my ancestors dance through me. In fact, an ex-boyfriend once saw me perform with my old dance group, and said that he saw me look more alive and happy than he had ever known me. He said it was as though I was on fire. I'm a passionate kinda gal, so that's saying something.

For at least a year when I was a child, the other children wouldn't hold my hands because I had warts on all my fingers. I would feel huge shame as those who danced on either side of me were told off (yet again) for not holding my hands. They would hold my little finger with the tips of theirs, as though they were being forced to touch a leper. But once the music started, and the dancing began, everything but this feeling of connectedness; of my heart and soul being on fire would disappear. The immigrant Serbs had created their ideal community based around their idea of what life in Serbia is about - it wasn't until I was in my mid 20s that I realised that the cool and hip youngsters of Serbia think that folk dancing is as outdated as we consider Morris dancing in England to be.

I danced as part of the group on and off until only last year - I left at the ripe old age of 43 years old. I ended up being the oldest female in the troupe. We would tour sometimes, in the UK, sometimes abroad. I missed out on the trips to the US, Australia and Serbia, but I danced in Claridges, a very posh hotel in London, to the King and Queen of Spain when I was 16. We were all served an amazing 3 course meal afterwards. It was the first time I was introduced to the concept of cold soup; our starter was Watercress and Cucumber Soup. I am still not convinced soup should be served cold.....

It was an easy transition for me to make to fall in love with rave music. The beats, breakbeats, piano tunes, fast fancy footwork........and even though I rarely did "ecstasy" the love drug associated with rave culture, there was something about the power of that connectedness, that feeling of euphoric love and oneness that kept me going back like an addict.......and once I had discovered it, there was no way my Mum could keep me locked in anymore. That was when the running away began.

People who didn't understand it thought it was just about people taking ecstasy; that it was about the drugs. No, it was about connection, and about love. A tribal desire to break free from the constraints of a society and political climate that did not understand love, community, connection, caring for one another. The drugs may have brought that out even more, but it was people's souls yearning for more love in the world that was the root to this near-revolution, politically, socially, and culturally.

It didn't matter where you were from, how much money you had, what your parents did, what you looked like.......the only thing that we cared about was whether everyone was HAPPY. Like Bhutan's measure of national success, which measures GDH (Gross Domestic Happiness) rather than GDP, we just wanted to know each and every other person was OK. The moment we saw someone who might not be, we would reach out and say "alright mate? You OK?", and stop and chat. A manifesto for life, I reckon - one that we wanted our politics to reflect, something we could see was missing.

And it really was a near-revolution. It was a HUGE shift in consciousness that threatened the political system. The Government brought in the Criminal Justice Act, as a way to break up the gathering of our tribe. Some say the Government deliberately flooded the rave scene with cocaine, to replace ecstasy, in order to bring a disconnection from that amazing connection to love people had.......moving them away from their hearts, to their egos.

It was a political reflection into the mirror of my life; what it meant to see a broken system; corrupt, uncaring, political structures designed to save the few and break the many. Ravers wanted to break free from the 1980s Thatcherite self-serving ideologies, and remember that none of us is an island, that we are all here together, as one family, and need love as the glue that binds us.

My absolute favourite band, as I mentioned at the beginning, are The Prodigy. I loved them sooooo much, and still do, and every time their tunes came on would delight in the atmosphere and energy and joy in the crowd. I very rarely did drugs myself. I would get so naturally high just on the music and the atmosphere, that I realised I didn't need them – and I didn't want to get to the stage that I needed drugs to be able to enjoy raving as I had seen happen to others.

A standard greeting was always "what are you on?" ....and answers would include any combination of pills, trips, speed and weed. Coke was rare (it was considered too moody). At every rave, without fail, I would be asked what I was on, and I would tell people I was on "a natural", and they wouldn't believe me. Such was the pull of the music to me, that I was known to wake from my half hour 3am nap, to go into full dancing mode in 5 seconds flat, which didn't help me persuade people I hadn't let a drug pass my lips.

Outside of the raves, in my everyday life, I couldn't listen to music at the same time as having a conversation with people – I kept having to pause the conversation as the music lifted me out of myself into some magic place in time and space where all is One. I still get like that now.

I didn't understand this at the time, but raving has always been a truly spiritual experience for me. A connection to love, humanity, and to the God in all things. Where everybody matters, where happiness is more important than money, where people care and feel freedom and joy. It was what kept me sane. It kept me happy. It gave my crazy tough life a purpose and me strength and something to look forward to. It gave me life.

12

When I first went to Manchester to see the University, it was for an open day. I knew – from the moment I had stepped off the train – that I had come home.

I didn't really work very hard for my A-Level exams, so it wasn't a surprise that I didn't actually get the results I needed to get into my Pharmacy degree. "Call Brighton, your second choice University, right away to make sure you've got a place" my Careers teacher had told me, as soon as I saw my exam results. "No" I told her. "I'm going to Manchester". She told me there was no point phoning them, that it would be a waste of my time, that I'd better call Brighton as quickly as possible to secure my place. But I knew. I knew I was going to Manchester because it was home. So I ignored the Careers Teacher's advice, and rushed to the one and only payphone in the school, the one I had called Social Services from a couple of years before, and called Manchester University. I still had a place. I was going.

This was 1993. The infamous Hacienda was in full swing, and Manchester (or Madchester as we lovingly called it) had a massive a hip and happening club and dance scene. I spent my first year living in Halls of Residence with 8 other girls. I used to go to lectures just to sleep off the club nights I had been at. I was in a nightclub 6 nights out of 7 every week, and I was in heaven.

I got involved very quickly with volunteering for a students' listening helpline service. This happened, like all of the best things in my life, by accident.

My flatmate Glenda, a brilliant Geordie lass whose strong accent no-one could understand except me, had decided she fancied someone at the Fresher's Fair, an event for new students to join different clubs and societies based on what they love doing. There are so many to choose from – from sports clubs to wine and cheese societies, to those for people from different parts of the world. The man Glenda fancied was on a stall for a society called "Nightline". Glenda loved clubbing as much as I did, and thought it was a society for people who loved clubbing at nighttime. She begged me to go with her to the Saturday meetup with her so that she could see him again. "OK then" I said.

Nightline, it turned out, was not a society for people who loved clubbing. It was a listening helpline service for students, a bit like the Samaritans. When we went to the Saturday meetup, we weren't talking about throwing shapes, tunes and dance moves. We were sitting in small groups discussing listening and basic counselling skills. Far from being disappointed, we LOVED it, and stayed for the 12 week training programme, passing our assessments to become volunteers with flying colours.

So I spent a lot of time at the Students' Union. I got to know lots of people quickly. I met a lovely guy who became my boyfriend. It amazed him that I could stand on the steps of the Students' Union and say hello to every 3rd person who walked by. That's a lot of people – Manchester University is a big place. I got to know so many people, and loved loved loved my life there. Lectures became a place to catch up on the sleep I wasn't having.

I had an amazing evening a couple of months after I had arrived at Manchester University. The Orb were playing at Manchester Academy, and a friend from the halls of residence who I didn't know that well, Dominic, had offered to go and get us tickets because he knew I wanted to go. The tickets sold out in a flash, but we'd been lucky. People had been offering me £20 for my £10 ticket, such was the desperation for people to go.

But I had a bit of a dilemma. Dominic had an LSD trip that he'd been given for his birthday, and offered to share it with me saying it wouldn't be fun doing it on his own. "OMG you've GOT to!" said Glenda, who had taken them before. "You'll be bloody brilliant!!!".

I was so bloody brilliant that I lost Dominic within half an hour of getting into the venue, and as soon as I came up on the acid trip, I just wanted to go and be with and talk to my friends. So I left to go and find them in the student bar, and missed The Orb completely.

By 3am, when I had exhausted all of my friends having taken them to each party in our Halls of Residence that night, at least 3 times, I had to come up with another plan. There was an "after Orb" party in a lads flat in the next block. "Right!" I thought. "I'll go there! I don't care if I'm going by myself!".

~

My room in Halls had a lovely wide window that would span 80% of the length of my room. The view out of it in the mornings was beautiful, with the most glorious sunrises to behold. Most students were lucky enough to do about 12 hours of lectures a week (some as little as 6!), so not many people were awake at dawn. But I'd usually been clubbing, so I was either up, ready to get dressed and get to my 9am science lectures, or was getting up after maybe a couple of hours' sleep. The first thing I would do when I got up was to open the curtains so I could see the beautiful view. Then I would go into the corner of the room where there was no window and get dressed. Sometimes I would realise that I had left my bra or another item of clothing on my chair at the other end of the room, and would tell myself that it was OK, no-one was awake anyway, and run over to get what I needed and run back to the corner to carry on dressing.

The after Orb party was in a ground floor flat in the next building. I could see their front room from my bedroom window, but it was too far away to actually see people in it. So off I went to the party, all acid-tripped up, ready to find more people to talk to.

When I walked in, I sat down next to a guy who was so stoned that he couldn't move. An inch.

"Where are you from?" he asked.

"Derby 17" I responded, telling him the name of my flat.

"What, is that that flat over there?" he asked, taking his time to move his hand, arm and finger at the speed of a sloth, eventually pointing out of the front room window in the general direction of my flat.

"Yes", I replied, delighted that he knew where I lived.

"It's really funny" he began. "There's this girl who keeps changing in the window, and we wish she wouldn't do it, because we keep being late for our lectures".

Alarm bells started to ring.

"What does she look like, do you know?" I asked. "No" came the reply.

The alarm bells continued to ring. So I made Mr Super Stoned Unable to Move get up, walk out of his flat, despite it being clearly a big effort for him to do. It was November and had started to snow outside.

"Show me" I told him. "Which room it is". He obliged. And, fuck me, he pointed to my room.

I could have got away with it. They didn't know what her face looked like, he said. But I have always been an honest soul, and honesty combined with drugs is sometimes endearing, but in this case, was a liability.

"FUCK! That's my room!" I shouted.

Mr Super Stoned Unable to Move actually broke into a run, in his effort to get back into his flat. "I've found her!" I could hear him shouting to everyone at the party. "I've found the girl who keeps changing in the windows!".

I spent the following 3 hours looking at pretty colours and shapes, whilst staring at the blank white breeze-block walls in my room. By myself. Too fucked to sleep, and too embarrassed to go anywhere else.

I had the best year of my life. I partied and danced, and laughed, and talked, and ran around Manchester on crazy adventures, doing amazing things, meeting brilliant people, having the time of my life. I was volunteering on a helpline that made me feel I was contributing in some way, that I could do something that helped others. I was free – and I was safe. For the first time in my life, I could relax. I was far from home, with no-one to follow me. But something else was happening in that safety. It had become safe enough to talk about my childhood. And training to become a Nightline volunteer had made me reflect on my life. So I also started to feel some of the pain.

It was no surprise that I failed my first year exams. I didn't do any revision. In fact, I didn't have many lecture notes because I had slept through so many of them. But I got my head down that summer, and stayed in Manchester on my own so I wouldn't be distracted by friends back home. I worked for Boots as an undergraduate Pharmacy Assistant in the day, and revised my socks off at night and weekends. It was a tough summer, I felt lonely, all my friends having gone home, and the Manchester I loved – student Manchester - had become a ghost town. I had become really quite depressed. I was already feeling suicidal, but I didn't allow myself to think about it too much. I kept pushing myself to study, knowing that things would be alright again once I'd passed my exams and made it into the second year. By the time the resits came, I was ready.

It was the Anatomy and Physiology exam where everything came crashing down. I turned over the exam paper, and looked at the questions. I was so happy seeing them, they were the perfect questions for me. I knew exactly what was needed, and could answer every question fully, I knew this was a paper I would easily pass. But I was tired from all the hard work and revision. I closed my eyes. When I opened them, I looked at the clock, and saw that 20 minutes had passed. "Shit!" I thought. "I've just slept through 20 minutes, will I have enough time to complete the paper?!".

And then it happened. I couldn't breathe. I couldn't think. I felt trapped inside my body, my heart pounding, my face feeling red and hot. Tears were pouring down my face, and I didn't know what to do, so I sat for another 10 long minutes trying to compose myself, hiding my tears with my long hair, before I realised I had to tell someone that I needed help.

Later that day, when my course friends came to find me, they said they all heard me wail outside the room in distress because I couldn't breathe. I had had my first ever panic attack. That was the end of any attempt to pass my resits, and that year.

The invigilators had tried to encourage me to calm down, and to go back in and finish the paper but I couldn't think. I left the building, and went to the nearest payphone and dialled my friend Shara's number., who I knew wasn't in an exam at the time. "Where are you?" she asked, panicked, when she worked out it was me on the other end. "Why aren't you in an exam?". The only words I could say were "I don't know". When she asked me where I was, I couldn't explain it to her, even though I was standing in a payphone outside the Students' Union, a place I had walked past at least twice a day for almost a year. "I don't know. I'm standing across the road from a bank. There is a post box next to me", was all I could manage. "Stay there. I'll come and find you" she said. And she did.

Shara, and some of my coursemates knew I wasn't right. The light had left my eyes.

I didn't know what I would do, or who I would be if I couldn't be a pharmacist. I had spent 5 years working Saturdays and holidays in a pharmacy, I knew my way around a dispensary, the indications and contraindications of all the drugs, like a pro. Being a pharmacist was my one-way ticket out of my life, to stability, money, status, respect, security, safety, an identity that everyone could relate to. Who I was, who I would be, my whole identity and my hope of a better life seemed to have vanished in a puff of smoke.

Shara came to see me the next day. I wouldn't - couldn't - get out of bed. So she did one of the most wonderful things. She took my duvet off me, walked down the stairs with it, and out of the front door. Standing in the middle of the road with my duvet, she shouted up to me "Come out now Dee! I am not bringing that duvet back in, so if you want it, you have to come out here to get it".

So I dragged myself down the stairs and out of the door and followed her to her place for the night.

And then devised a plan.

On the way back to mine the next day, I went via a pharmacy, and bought a load of paracetamol tablets. I was going to say goodbye.

This wasn't the time I was sent back, but I was definitely saved. This was my second suicide attempt. My first attempt at 15 years old was taking 20 aspirin. I never told anyone what I had done. My cousin phoned me the next day and frantically said 'What's the matter? Ever since last night I keep seeing you and an ambulance. Something is wrong with you, I know it". I asked her what time she had started to see the ambulance. She said 8pm. That was the time I had started to take the pills. She'd tried to call all evening, but my Mum had been on the phone so she couldn't get through. It was a really profound moment for me realising that angels come not just from the heavens but exist in life too, and there is more to life than what we see with our physical eyes.

On this occasion, my second attempt, I took over 60 paracetamol tablets washed down with cider and black(currant).

I later wrote an anonymous account of that suicide attempt for the Nightline suicide training session, as a way of trying to help volunteers understand what it can feel like. In writing this book, I have found it again, and wonder it it's helpful to share what was happening for me. I wrote this when I was 19 years old. This is what it says:

"I had been suicidal for a couple of months before I finally felt that my suicide bid was justified. Those two months were the longest months that I have ever experienced. Every night I would pray that I would die in my sleep, only to wake up every morning feeling the same misery at being alive. Everyday tasks like work, shopping, cooking, staying in touch with people I love were so difficult. I don't know how I managed to get up in the mornings, knowing that all the upsetting events occurring around me were not just a nightmare but a reality.

I kept telling myself that I had to keep going, that things would eventually improve. And most importantly, I felt that I couldn't put my friends and family through coping with my death. Even though I felt totally miserable, I couldn't inflict that misery onto them. And I felt unable to tell anyone how bad I felt because I felt silly and embarrassed for feeling so low. I also didn't want to burden them with my troubles.

Then, one morning, I realised that I just couldn't – wouldn't - take any more. I was in my own separate bubble and I could see the world going on around me outside of my bubble, but I didn't feel a part of it.

That morning, I realised that I couldn't keep myself alive against my will, even to spare upsetting my friends and family. Eventually after their anger and guilt had lessened, I felt that my friends and family would understand why I had to go. Maybe some of them would be happy for me to finally be at peace. So now it was OK for me to die.

I felt relieved. Much happier than I had in a very long time. I was still in my bubble, as I went for a little walk, and I found that all I could think of was how I would take my life. Every time I crossed a road, all I could see was a fast car that could run me over. But no, I couldn't inflict that on the driver. Or the building that I could leap off. But how would I get to the roof?

I decided to take an overdose. That way I could at least write an explanation and try to apologise to my friends and family, once I got home.

With every tablet I swallowed, I felt better, closer to a happier, more peaceful place. The doorbell rang several times while I was taking the tablets. The telephone rang constantly. But I didn't respond. What if someone had guessed what I was up to, by my voice or my appearance? I would be stopped. They'd try to convince me that I was being stupid, that things would get better. They wouldn't understand. I couldn't handle being talked out of it. I had made up my mind; I knew that things couldn't improve, so I was going somewhere else where things would be better.

I thought that I would fall asleep, and would pass away easily enough in my sleep. But the tablets made me ache, all the muscles in my body were going into spasm. I threw up. So I took more tablets. And worst of all, I couldn't sleep."

~

When someone takes a paracetamol overdose, there is a window of 4 hours during which someone's stomach can be pumped, and/or charcoal given. After that, they have to be put on a Parvolex drip, which attempts to block the liver receptors from taking up any more paracetamol until it's cleared from the body. Hospital pharmacists apparently hate making it up, because it smells of rotting eggs. This needs to be ideally started within 8 hours of the overdose. No-one speaks about this, but it takes 2-3 days for someone to die from a paracetamol overdose, and its excruciatingly painful. Each organ slowly shuts down. And there are no painkillers that can be taken at that point to ease the process of dying. It's a slow agonising death. It doesn't actually take that much paracetamol to trigger a fatal overdose, yet we can buy them as easily as sweets. As a pharmacy student, I knew how many to take to be 100% certain I would die. I just didn't know it would hurt so much.

7 hours after I had taken the overdose, I was in agony. I was writhing in pain on my bedroom floor. I was desperate for the pain to stop. I was still committed to dying, and wanted to, but this was ridiculous. I didn't expect it to hurt so much. So I told one of my housemates what I had done, not because I wanted to stop dying, but because I wanted the pain to stop.

I was really lucky not to have been put on a psychiatric ward. That would, most definitely, have tipped me over another edge entirely. I think the nurses and doctors knew this, and deliberately kept me on the medical ward to prevent this. I was in hospital for 5 days. 3 days after I had been admitted to hospital, a nurse came and gently sat on the end of my bed, and spoke to me.

"We've all been chatting about you. We know that you meant it. You wouldn't be studying to be a pharmacist and have done this if you didn't mean it. We know this wasn't a cry for help.". I started to cry. I told the nurse some of what had been happening. I felt my despair and let her see it. I don't remember her name, but I will forever be grateful to her. She made me feel truly seen and heard, probably for the first time in my whole life. I felt held, truly held, also probably for the first time in my whole life. She arranged some help for me, and I was supported to look at my options.

Manchester University agreed that I could resit my first year, but I wasn't allowed to attend the lectures with any of the new first years because I wasn't paying fees for the year, just attending the examinations. I was disappointed by this – I wanted to apply myself and get some really good notes, and actually pay attention this time around. I was a good student when I applied myself, and I wanted to do the best I could.

So I got to have one more year in one of my favourite cities. I was 19 years old. The cracks were starting to show. But I was happy and grateful to have been given another chance.

13

Just after I had been released from hospital, there was a meeting for Nightline volunteers who wanted to get more involved, taking on Committee position to help run it. There were several teams, including the social team, and the marketing team, and the training team, the finance and admin team. Meetings were held for each team at the same time, just in different rooms on the same floor of the Students' Union building.

I can't remember what I wanted to do, it definitely wasn't training volunteers. That sounded terrifying. I think it was probably being a part of the social team.

But I wasn't paying attention properly to where I was going, and ended up in the "wrong" meeting. 19 years old, fresh out of hospital having tried to kill myself, and too embarrassed to tell anyone that I was in the "wrong" room, I ended up a member of the training team.

Two weeks later, I was facilitating a discussion with 60 new volunteers, using a flipchart to write down ideas for what "good" and "bad" counselling skills look like. I was convinced everyone could see the elephant-sized piles of poo forming behind me, I was so scared. But I LOVED it all at the same time. I felt alive, like I had a purpose, and could make a difference in a really positive way. I was doing something that, it turned out, I was really really good at.

Of course I now look back and realise I wasn't in the "wrong" room at all. I found myself a little through becoming a trainer, and doing something in which I flourished – and helped others to flourish too.

Very quickly I became the joint lead trainer along with the man who became my boyfriend. We became known for being amongst the best Nightline trainers in the country – we were like training Gods; the stuff of legends.

We walked volunteers through exercises that made them explore the greatest and most painful life circumstances that callers might have faced. We prepared them to deal with calls from people who had been abused, who had been bereaved, who were HIV positive, who were gay or lesbian, people who felt suicidal. In the early 90s, being gay or HIV positive was still such a taboo, so we were doing deep and profound work, taking the volunteers on a deep and personal journey to accept themselves, so that they could accept others and truly listen. Our exercises were profound, and moving, and watching our volunteers realise what they were capable of, literally watching them transform before our eyes.....well, this was and still is one of the most wonderful feelings in the world to me. To see others grow and have eureka moments, is like watching magic to me. I loved it. I still love teaching and training now for the very same reason – seeing people grow into the greatest they can be is some of the most beautiful, wonderful magic there is to me.

I continued to have an amazing time, but I also knuckled down and started to study much harder. I think my challenge was that I was having to do all the learning by myself, like doing a distance learning course from my textbooks, but I tried my best. I got a job at The Friendship Inn, a pub across the road from Platt Fields. And I started to see a counsellor at the University Counselling Service, who helped me start exploring the traumas of my childhood. She was wonderful and I loved our sessions. I wanted to learn everything I could and grow.

But I still had fun, and clubbed and danced and partied and laughed and laughed and laughed, spending most of my time at my boyfriend's flat in his halls of residence, with the lads he lived with, some of whom were some of the funniest people I have ever met.

19 of us travelled together to Blackpool for my 20th birthday, we had the best time. Old school friends had made the trip up especially.

My then boyfriend worked as a bouncer at the student bar in his halls of residence, and sat on the resident's committee. So I got to – yet again – know everyone. We had so much fun.

One night, Hugh Lennon and his Hypnotic Dog performed a stage hypnotic show at the residents' bar. I knew every one of the 300 people in the audience. When Hugh asked for volunteers to be hypnotised for the show, I was happy to put my hand up, and got to share the stage with several other people, including my good friend Richard. It was hilarious.

I was told, under hypnosis, that I could translate Martian, and proceeded to do just that with someone who had been told they actually were a Martian. I had been told that the number 7 didn't exist, and so proceeded to count in all manner of ways, always missing out the number 7.

You know those laughs of hilarity where people are stuggling to breathe in between the tears pouring down their faces?

I knew that those laughs from the audience were because of what I was doing when Hugh played "Like a Virgin" by Madonna. I knew that none of the other ladies on the stage were doing anything that was making them laugh as much as I was. But, in a hypnotic state, I didn't feel any shame, or self-consciousness, or embarrassment at what I was doing. I was just doing what I had been asked to do, whilst under hypnosis. Which was to imitate Madonna when her song came on the PA system.

The thing was, I didn't know much about Madonna. I had loved *Vogue*, but wasn't a massive fan like some of my friends were. I was a raver. Madonna was not big on the raving scene. The only thing I really knew about her was that she'd just gone on tour and controversially simulated masturbating during her set. I only knew about it because it was all over the papers. I had never even discovered the joys of self-pleasure at that point in my life, and my sexual expression was always very private between me and my boyfriend. But I had been asked to imitate Madonna, and that was all I really knew about her. And the shame / self-consciousness filter had been switched off thanks to Hugh Lennon and his Hypnotic Dog.

So the fun I had continued that year, but I definitely got a lot more sleep, and actually studied.

I worked really really hard. I would spend my days revising in the coffee shop in the Students' Union, a place I loved to learn. And so I have no idea why I failed my exams again. Actually, that's not strictly true. I do know why. I wasn't meant to be pharmacist. I just couldn't understand it at the time; I was bright enough, had worked hard that year, I had checked, double checked and triple checked every exam paper when I had finished and was convinced that this time I had passed everything. But it wasn't meant to be.

I was more accepting of my failure this time around, but it was still a painful process deciding what to do next. My other love was Psychology – I loved people, and have always been fascinated by why we do the things we do – inspired by my mother and father. But University places had all been allocated for the following year. In the end, I had a choice of 2 places of study – Bolton Institute of Higher Education or the University of Kent at Canterbury. Choosing Bolton would have meant I could have stayed living in Manchester.

"But what would an employer do," my boyfriend said to me. "if they were choosing between a candidate with a degree from Bolton Institute of Higher Education and another one from The University of Kent at Canterbury? Who would they choose?".

I knew I had to go to Canterbury.

14

"What's it like?" my friends and boyfriend would ask me. "Beautiful" was what I would reply.

That's all I could say. Canterbury is stunning. But it had one nightclub. And for a raver from London, who'd spent 2 years partying in Manchester, away from her friends and boyfriend, with no money and having to work as much as possible to pay extra fees for University, having already failed one attempt at a degree, the cracks just got bigger and bigger.

Going to Canterbury was, in all honesty, a shock. My housemates were amazing, and I made some great friends. But it was so quiet, and so still, that my pain started to bubble up and the noise of my life had gone quiet so I couldn't hide from or ignore my memories anymore. I could hear my own thoughts, and feel my own feelings of trauma that I had suppressed or ignored for a lifetime and the pain of it all was kicking in.

15

My 21st birthday was on the 7th of March 1996. I had decided to celebrate it back up in Manchester, with my boyfriend and all my friends up there. I was sooooo excited, and it had given me something to really look forward to. It was what had kept me going, because I had found myself stuck in a rut. I loved my studies, but felt like a failure. I missed my boyfriend and my friends. I missed the music and the dancing, and the buzz, and the energy of being in a bustling, happening city where I was part of something. It was a place I truly belonged.

Something else was happening too. The safety I felt in Manchester, being so very very far away from home, and away from my father, wasn't with me anymore. Canterbury was within easy travelling distance for him, and I didn't feel safe. When he made an attempt to contact me and find out where I was, I contacted the University and told them my circumstances. They took my safety very seriously, and immediately issued notices that my personal details were not to be revealed to anyone, not even my immediate family members, especially not to my father.

So, 6 months after I had first arrived in Canterbury, I got myself on a train, hugely excited to be heading up to the one place I loved the most. My home in my heart, Manchester.

16

It was the night before my 21st birthday that my boyfriend told me the news. He had started seeing the new trainer on the Nightline training team. We were over. I don't remember much about my trip other than feeling this incredible pain. He wasn't my first serious boyfriend, but this felt different. I can't remember now whether we had talked about getting engaged or I had imagined it, but this felt like a much more meaningful relationship than my previous two, so it really hurt. I also felt in that trip that the Danica-shaped-hole in Manchester had shrunk somehow. That my time there, and my connection to the place where I had been happiest was vanishing. I didn't love Canterbury, I felt bored, and disconnected and unsafe. I felt I had nothing left to hold on to.

I had never really confided in my Mum about anything too serious, because she was really quite traditional, and also because she couldn't really cope with me needing her. She wanted me to need her, but I knew couldn't cope with the emotions that this would bring up. She had always needed me, and I had always needed to be strong for her.

But I was broken. Once I was back in Canterbury, I phoned her and poured my heart out about how sad I was, how upset I was about the split, and how it had happened. It was the only time I really truly let myself share what was in my heart. And my Mum was wonderful. Really truly wonderful. She listened, and empathised, and was everything I had ever wished she could be to me. Above all, she was so very grateful to me for opening up to her. I could feel her relief that we could talk in this way. And that relief led to something else. An edge I wished she hadn't gone to.

When the words came, I knew it meant things were not now going to be OK. "Watch the news carefully", she had said at the end of our chat. "You'll see, there will be a bomb reported on the news tonight. Trust me. There's a bomb about to go off".

She was about to have another psychotic breakdown. That's what those words meant. And it was happening because I had finally let my Mum in, confided in her, and she had had an overwhelming experience of relief, that we could be really close once more. Too overwhelming in fact.

It meant I was needed again. To go home, and look after my Mum, and stay awake for a week trying to contain her psychosis and the constant craziness that went with it, and make sure my little sister was OK.

I just couldn't do it. I was exhausted by my life. I couldn't be strong for my Mum anymore, and strong in my life, when my life was full of pain and sorrow and failure and hurt and abuse and trauma. My beloved raving had gone, the music and dancing had stopped, I had lost my connection to all that brought me joy and happiness. I felt I had nothing left to give and nothing left to enjoy. So I decided that this was it; that it was time to go now. It was OK to do so, I'd given it my best shot. I started to plan my next steps.

2 weeks after my 21st birthday, I was back in Manchester, and ready to leave for good.

17

It's apparently quite common to feel how I felt as I was preparing once I had made my decision. I became detached emotionally and went back into the same bubble I had entered before my last overdose. I was very clear and focused on ensuring that I followed through with my decision.

Psychiatrists and psychologists the world over would say that we have to be depressed to be suicidal, but I always felt that I actually wasn't depressed. Not this time around. I had made the decision to leave because I was exhausted by my life, and, actually, having made the decision to die, I found this immense peace and stillness.

My senses became heightened. It was like I could hear the birds singing more clearly, and noticed the wind on the trees more than I normally would have. Life took on a preciousness, and I was absorbing, through my senses, every moment around me as though it was my last chance to do so. I wanted to savour every moment of the world around me. I saw and felt the world as a beautiful place, but just a place in which I no longer wanted to be, in a life that was not beautiful for me.

In the end, it was actually quite a logical decision to me.

I started to feel disconnected from the world, as though I were a visitor – a tourist from another planet. I no longer felt that I belonged here, that this planet was my home. I became an observer of the world I was in rather than an active participant. I couldn't relate to people living their normal lives. I felt an immense sense of calm and purpose. Nothing was going to change my mind. Where I was going felt good. I was at peace.

I made two phone calls before I boarded the train to Manchester, to say goodbye. One was to one of my oldest schoolfriends. She was starting to get ready to revise for her final University exams, and I am not sure she ever truly forgave me for this. I genuinely wanted her to know that I loved her and how grateful I was to her for having been in my life. The second was to the boyfriend who had cheated on me. I'd like to say that it was for loving reasons. But it wasn't. It was a "fuck you bastard" moment. Of course I didn't say that to him, but I wanted him to feel like shit. I am not proud of this, but I feel it important to be honest and own that I wasn't coming from a good place in calling him.

I had taken a bed sheet, and cut it into strips. One I got to the park, I tied the ends together to make a really long strip of material.

I took every penny I had out of my bank account. It was enough to buy a one-way ticket to Manchester, and one really good meal before I died. I don't remember anything about the journey apart from feeling really connected to something bigger, and being very much in my bubble.

When I got to Manchester, I got myself a really big Chinese meal. I savoured every mouthful, every moment of flavour. My senses were still really heightened, so I was experiencing the meal in a way that I wasn't familiar with. Now I would call it mindfulness. I went into a state of mindfulness. Every moment mattered, every step I took, every breath I took mattered and was precious and I was experiencing the fullness of it all.

I waited until about 8pm, when it was dark, to take myself to Platt Fields. I don't remember how I entered the park, I think it had padlocked gates. Maybe there was a bend in one of the railings that meant I could just about squeeze through.

But I found myself in the park. I thought I would hang myself from a tree, but as I looked around, all I could see were trees whose branches were just too high up for me to reach. So I kept walking through the park until I could find somewhere or something suitable.

And then I saw it. A shelter with rafters next to the boating lake. As I sit here writing this, I have just pulled up a map of the park. I didn't know this until now, but the boating lake is heart shaped. How poetic and beautiful is that?!

Was I scared? Yes I was. I was calm and peaceful, but also knew that – despite my belief that I was going to a better place – I didn't actually 100% *know* where I was going. I couldn't *guarantee* that it was all I was imagining it would be. On some level I felt that, because I'd committed, because I'd made those calls, because I had *decided* I just had to go through with it, no matter what.

And as you will have read earlier, it was the third attempt at sitting down that did it. I was in a place of bliss. It felt amazing. Truly, deeply, profoundly wonderful. I saw a bright Light that spun above me and felt a peace unlike anything that I had ever even come close to in my life. I surrendered to that light and to that incredible peace. It was beautiful.

It took many years later for me to discover what had happened in that time and place, and how and why I was sent back. Why I came back.

19

As I passed into Spirit, I found myself in a large space that was a beautiful pale yet warm pastel pink colour. It didn't really have walls, but there was definitely an outer layer, a kind of giant soft bubble. It was this bubble that was this beautiful pink colour. Interlaced with it were wisps of a lovely pale warm blue colour in places. These colours weren't fixed, they were slowly moving, gently swirling. I felt very safe, even though it was a large place.

A being was walking towards me. He was tall and graceful. He looked like he must be from the stars, with huge almond shaped eyes. He didn't speak to me, just put out his right hand, and invited me to take it. Even though he wasn't speaking, I felt that he was speaking with me telepathically, welcoming me. It's like I could feel what he was saying, but no words had come out of his mouth. He had a beautiful blue energy about him.

"You will have some healing first", he said gently. "Before you go to speak with the Angel. Come over here".

He led me to a kind of antechamber to the left. It was a small room, still a warm shade of pink, but a little more muted, which made it a little cosier than the big entrance hall I had gone into. Again it felt very safe to be there, and beautiful. There was a bed, a bit like a massage couch there, and it was made of rose quartz crystal. It was perfectly my size. The being motioned for me to get onto the bed, and so I did. Even though the bed was fully imbued with the energy of rose quartz, it wasn't a hard bed, it felt soft, and I felt fully supported. Another being that looked like she came from the stars, with a beautiful yellow energy was there, and she looked down over me, smiling warmly at me, and then touched me on my third eye. I fell into a deep and beautiful, and tremendously peaceful sleep. I know that during this sleep a number of beings from the stars, and some angels had gathered, and were doing healing work on me. It's like they were repairing my aura, I could see them literally sowing it back together using a beautiful golden magical thread. It felt like I stayed there for a very long time. They worked with my heart, clearing the pain that I felt within it. I could see them lifting it out of my chest to heal it, before gently putting it back. My broken soul was soothed, repaired, made whole again.

And then once they had finished, they left me to rest for some time longer until I was ready to sit up. The yellow being came in as soon as I had awakened, to check if I was OK, and greeted me with the loveliest, warmest, most caring smile. It felt wonderful.

I was then given a kind of meal.....something to consume, which – as I had it was, like I was being nourished from the inside out. The yellow being stayed with me and sat with me, just smiling beautifully and warmly, making sure I was OK.

Once I had finished, and felt like it was time for the next step, she asked me if I was ready to go on. I said yes. I felt completely calm and at peace. I think it felt a bit weird because I was expecting to see more souls, I guess. There was an emptiness to where I was. But I was curious about what was coming next, so didn't think about it for too long.

I followed the yellow being, and then found myself somewhere that was all completely white. Everything was white. I couldn't see an end, or walls, or an enclosure – or limits. It was just all white.

An angel was sat on what looked like a big white log. There was another big white log next to it. He was all in white, and looked really very beautiful. He had a calmness to him, but there was a seriousness to his expression. He looked at me, smiling, and motioned for me to sit on the other white log.

"Danica", he said, pronouncing my name in perfect Serbian. "You can't come through". It was at this point I became aware that far away were colourful shadows of other souls. Some were waiting, watching, others were walking past. I couldn't see who or what they were, and it felt like I would be unable to reach them.

"It's not your *right time*", he continued with the same serious yet kind expression.

"But!" I started to protest. Thanks to having been born feisty, I was never one to put off challenging an injustice, and not even the presence of an angel would deter me. "Erm....are you kidding? Can you just have a look and see what I just did there?! That took real effort to get myself here!".

So the angel – Archangel Metatron, in fact – said:

"Good effort.......but there's something else we need you to do now."

I felt my heart sinking.

Archangel Metatron then moved his hand in a slight swirling motion, and in so doing, created a floating vision of my life on Earth. It was a bit like watching my life on a TV screen, but everything was all a bit floaty, like watching it on a cloud. As I looked into this vision cloud, I was really struck by the bright colours of watching my life, the greens were the brightest greens, the blues the brightest blues, the reds the deepest reds. It was like the story of me and my life on Earth had had an extra layer of colourisation added to it – a bit like digital remastering, I supposed. He talked me through what I was seeing.

I was being shown my life on Earth, were I to return.

Archangel Metatron talked me through the different experiences I had agreed I would have. He explained that the following 20 or so years would be hard, that I would still have fun, but that they would hard on me too.

"You agreed you would go through this, for in this journey you chose wisdom as your soul's calling, and wisdom comes from experience. You will use your wisdom later to great effect for the benefit of humankind, but your experiences are necessary first to help you get there", he explained. "It needed not to have been so difficult", he carried on. "But you chose this for this lifetime."

As I looked at the vision cloud, he showed me the experiences that were to come.

The angel explained, as I watched it all on the cloud, that soon after my return, my mother would fall sick with cancer, that the process of her developing cancer had already begun. He explained that I would nurse her, and care for her, and that she would eventually die. He explained that it would be very painful for me, and I would experience a huge sense of loss. I would have to care for my young sister, and my slightly younger brother for a while, and it would be hard.

"This loss will bring you the wisdom of bereavement. It will connect you spiritually to the heavens, for you will see your Mum and speak with her. She will visit you in your dreams, and then one day she will speak with you while you are walking and you will know she is by your side, just separated by the thin veil that separates human life from spiritual life. She will become your greatest teacher for a while, and guide you. She will be funny too, she will keep her personality cloak for you to recognise her, and to make you and your friends laugh. Her personality gifts from this life were always endearing, so those she will keep. For you."

I was shown my future first husband, who I was to meet shortly after her funeral. "He is a gift to you, for that time. Not always, but for then. He will help you find a peace and a stillness and a calm that will be and is needed in your life." I was shown a vision of him greeting me, the first time I saw him in his office at work after we had got together. The way he turned to me, with wonderful smiling eyes, a great big wide smile, standing up from his chair with his arms outstretched, ready to greet me, delighted to see me. I could see his office clearly, the books on the bookshelves.

Later, back on the Earth, I had always thought that I had seen this vision of my first husband in a dream, because I recognised the vision when I went to see him that first time after we'd got together. Now I know it wasn't a dream – I was seeing what this angel had shown me in the vision cloud.

"He will make you happy for a time, but that time will end too." Said the angel.

He then showed me the heartbreak that would come from our split. I was shown how an ex-girlfriend of his would get in touch and take him off to a new life, away from me. It would be agony. Literally like a soul being split in two.

"It will be agonising", the angel said. "For a long, long, long, long time you will feel so much pain in your heart. But also you will get over it. Eventually." He said matter-of-factly.

"Why....?" I began, but the angel read my mind, and knew that my question was why I would have chosen this experience.

"To experience heartbreak", came the answer. "You will be ever so slightly smug in your happiness in this relationship, and this [experience] will give you compassion for others' pain. So you can understand them when they come to you so that you can help them", he added.

I took a breath.

And then I was shown the father of my child. How I would see an angel intervene to ensure he could be conceived, that he was a beautiful, wonderful, bright and brilliant boy. "Just like you, Danica", said the angel, smiling.

He then talked me through the unfolding visions of my sadness and unhappiness at realising that I wasn't in the right relationship for me, splitting up from my son's father whilst pregnant, agonising over a decision about where to live; in Sheffield or Brighton. I was shown I would move to Brighton, together with his father for a very short time, but that we would split very soon after my son's birth.

I could see the tears that would pour down my face, and the misery that would engulf me in the form of post-natal depression. I was shown how I would stand gazing in through coffee shop windows, wondering which happy smiling mother I should give my child to, to give him a better start in life than I felt I could provide for him.

"But you will be happy", said the angel. "This isn't where it ends". I was shown the joy that my son would bring me, the glints of sunshine and moments of happiness that would fight their way through my life experience, one of struggle and pain on the outside. "But you will feel happiness also", he said once more.

"And this is what will carry you through", he said. "*Your* personality. *Your* tenacity. *Your* sense of irreverence, fun and joy. It's no accident it's woven into the very fabric of Who You Are", he said, smiling.

"So what next?" I asked.

"They will be very hard on you, those years when he is small. He [the child's father] will bully you and hate you and make your life hard. You will have to go to Court for the silliest of things. It will be agony for you. You won't have much money.".

"Why......?" came the question again.

"Because you will help others in similar situations", he replied. "Because you have to see it first before you can. Wisdom. Building yet more wisdom again."

And then I was shown the fun times I would have. Going to Glastonbury Festival, dancing, being out with my friends. I was shown the vegan organic cake business I would attempt. I was shown how much spark my personality carries, the laughter, the cheekiness, the feistiness, the fun. I was shown key people in my life who would help me laugh and smile and dance and just carry on. I was shown some of the amazing, dear wonderful friends my life would be graced with whose sense of humour matched my own. "And *this* one", he said, pointing to my friend Amanda, "her laugh is infectious". (It so is, my dude and I reckon it's the best laugh in the world). I was shown the boy I would end up "accidentally" nannying. "He will be like a son to you", said the angel. His mother is one of my dearest friends and soulsisters.

"Remember, Danica, you are gathering wisdom, through your experiences during this lifetime, because it will come to serve you and others later".

I was shown that, at some point in my early 40s my life would change. I would eventually become friends with my son's dad, and we would know peace.

And then I was shown a wonderful gift I would be given. A relationship of such fun, and brilliance, and depth and connection and pure happiness. I was shown the happy life we would live. "This one stays with you", said the angel.

"But why can't I stay now?" I asked. "I want to stay now. I made the effort to come."

And then I was shown again that there was something I had promised to do. That I would help humanity in some way. I still don't know what that is because I can't remember that bit of it at all. It's like I wasn't allowed to remember that part of the conversation when it came round, there's like a haze in front of my memory of it. A veil. I think it's supposed to be a surprise.

"So", said the angel, looking down at me, warmly smiling.

"Knowing everything that you know, having seen everything that you have been shown, will you go back?".

"Yes", I replied.

It doesn't feel like it was a true choice to be honest, and I wonder what would have happened had I said no, but it was presented as a choice.

"Right then", he said, standing up. "Danica, it's time". We hugged. I felt so filled with peace and a beautiful loving white light. I felt loved. I felt the same deep beautiful peace I felt as I had passed into the spinning Light I saw at the start of my journey to this place.

"You'll be alright, dear one. Loved and happy." were the last words I heard.

And then it was dark again. And cold. I was standing in a park. In Manchester. Being gently guided away.

20

Since Keith Flint from The Prodigy hanged himself, I have been reflecting on this a lot.

I have been wondering if Keith was offered that same choice when he hanged himself. He famously gave an interview to NME in 2015 where he said that when he was done, he'd probably kill himself. For the week after he died, I kept hearing "I did it my way" by Frank Sinatra in my head......he really did do it his way.

My very human wish had been that he'd been sent back too, because I think we need him and his brilliant energy, kindness, two fingers to a system that we are dismantling that doesn't know love. And I had never even met him in person, so goodness knows what his family and bandmates and friends have gone through.

My guess is, had he been offered the choice to come back, he would've said, as a dear friend suggested, "Nah. Fuck that shit".

At least I hope that's what he would have said.

I would like to say that I came back and skipped on happily through my life, knowing that it would be alright in the end.

But that's not how it's been. I didn't know for many years about what had happened when I had passed over, about the conversation I had with the angel. There have been times when the exhaustion and pain and agony that I have felt with the unfolding events in my life, despite being a naturally happy dancing soul in my heart, have felt overwhelming. There have been times when I have wanted again just to pass over in my sleep, to not have to face yet another day. In those moments, since learning what happened in my passing, I have been known to laugh, using a dark humour that my Serbian roots blessed me with. "I'm not even allowed to fucking kill myself! The fuckers will send me back!"

I have often reflected on how, having been shown what happened when I passed over, I wasn't greeted by loved ones as I understand happens when people pass over. I know because I have seen this in another way.

Two nights before My Mum died, I didn't get a wink of sleep. I don't remember my Mum waking up in the night, as she had been doing, with attacks of shingles she'd developed. What I do remember is the house being full of people. Well, spirits. In fact, it sounded like there was a party going on. All I could see were brown sepia shadowy outlines of "people" – spirits – walking everywhere. In and out of the front room, up and down the stairs, in and out of my Mum's room, in and out of the kitchen. The level of noise was phenomenal. All I could hear were Serbian greetings of "Ah! Great to see you! How are you doing?! What have you been up to?!" – they were all behaving as though they hadn't seen each other in a while and had all been off doing their own thing. I wondered if I was hallucinating because of the lack of sleep and exhaustion of being a carer whilst working full time. No matter what I did to bring myself round to the present, they stayed. And carried on partying. In the end I went to lie back down to try to go to sleep, and then I saw my Deda - my Mum's dad who had died when she was 10 – and he was in full colour, in a navy blue suit, a white shirt and a red tie. He walked from the hallway, into the front room to where I was on the sofabed, bent over me as if to give me a kiss, and then stood up and walked through the wall into my Mum's room.

I couldn't allow myself to think about it afterwards, because I would have known what I had seen. That my Mum's ancestors and guides and angels had gathered to help her pass. I wasn't ready or able to know that this was coming. But the moment I knew she had died, I understood what I had seen and heard and felt. Her welcoming party.

I didn't get a welcoming party. It's another way I just know it wasn't my time. I think those colourful shadows in the background that I knew I wouldn't reach were the spirits in the heavens. But I think I was met in a place between this world and that one, a "middle world", if you like, a waiting room, through which I would not pass. Not then, anyway.

It is now 23 years since I passed over, and I can honestly say that I am really happy with my life, and have been for some time. It's taken me a long long time to get to this point. I hope that the lessons my life have taught me enrich those who come to my courses or read what I share. I am, as I write this, half-way through my studies to become a homeopath and have published a theory about medicine. My dude is a wonderful, brilliant, gorgeous young man who I am incredibly proud of, and his dad and I are finally developing a friendship. I still go raving, and dancing and party, and sometimes my knees have to remind me that I can dance on a podium for hours if I want to, but my body isn't 17 anymore. I swear like a trooper, and yet can be as still as peace itself when with the angels I work with. My life is rich in friendship and love.

My journey so far has taught me a lot, and I will continue to learn for the rest of my days, as I believe that we all do, if we allow our hearts to remain open and our souls free.

Most of all, I think, what I have learned is that, if we are here, alive, then we have a purpose in being here. We may not always feel it. I am reminded again of people living on the streets, many of whom I can imagine won't feel a purpose at all. But even they do. I really believe that they are angels calling us up to be the best that we can be. To help lift them off the streets. To create a world where each person is valued, has a home, healthy organic food, access to life-supporting healthcare that does no harm, and is a valued member of a community. To create a world where everyone is loved.

In these times and days of uncertainty in our world, there is one thing I always know is true. The Light is stronger than the darkness. I really believe it is our job to be that Light. To stand together, to help one another, to be one family – which we are. To move beyond the illusion of separation and realise and feel that we are all One. To love one other with our whole hearts. And to love our world; our home, and all the plants and animals and trees that live on her. To speak up for love, to say no to all that isn't love, to be brave and share what we know to be true about building a life of love on this Earth for everyone.

And that, when it is our time to pass, that our life – however long or short lived it may be – is *celebrated.* That we come to a greater peace around death, understanding that we may have chosen a long or a short life, a happy or sad one, but that when it is our time, it is our time. And if it isn't our time, then we'll be sent back if we try to pass through too soon. But if we are allowed through, however young, it is because it's time. We've been allowed through.

My experience taught me that I guess I am supposed to be here, right now, as I breathe. I believe the same is true of you.

We are supposed to be here, in all of our glory and magnificence. Our lives – even in those times when we can't feel it – mean something. We matter and we have a purpose. That purpose may simply be to live this adventure that we have chosen – and it may also be to interweave our lives and personalities and who we are with the lives of all around us. When we leave this Earth it is because our time is done, at whatever age that might be. We have had our experiences and shared what we have agreed to share with those who love us and it is time to move on.

There is a reason and a purpose to our being here. We make a difference. We matter. We will dance with the stars in the heavens one day, but for now, we are dancing stars on the Earth.

More Lessons I Learned

As well as everything I have shared so far, there are some additional reflections that I have, based on my experiences, which I hope are helpful.

Birth, Death & Suicide

I am going to share some ancient wisdoms on birth and death, and what these wisdoms might mean in terms of suicide, that have really inspired me to look at life differently. But before I do, I just want to get practical about what to do if you or someone you know feels suicidal.

Suicidal feelings

If you have any suicidal feelings at any time, I would say firstly, and most importantly – **please talk to someone.** There is *always* a way out of how we feel, out of our life situations, even if we can't see how ourselves at the time. Life can be really bloody hard, and tiring, but let me tell you something.

If it isn't your time, you won't be allowed through, so you might as well take a deep breath, tell yourself there is, or will be a way forward at some point, even if you don't know what it is right now, and ask that the people who can help you are sent to you. Ask for a miracle. I could write a whole other book just on the miracles I have seen, maybe that's one for another time. In the meantime, know that anything is possible.

But most importantly **ask for help**.

What can you do to help a friend or loved one who is feeling suicidal?

It's really hard watching someone you love and care about suffer. There are some really simple things that we can all do that can, and really do help and make a difference. I am not a mental health professional however, and professional help may be needed. This is based on my own personal experiences of what has helped me when I have felt suicidal.

1) Listen. Let your loved one talk without interruption.

2) Allow yourself to sit in the silence. Healing and releasing and transformation usually happen in those moments when we are still and silent, when the tears can just flow, the pain can just be felt, free from interruption. It's hard to be still, but one of the most wonderful and helpful things you can do is to just *be* with the person. You don't have to talk. The suicidal person knowing they aren't alone, that there is someone with them is one of the greatest gifts. You don't *have* to talk, just being there really *IS* enough – and actually the best thing you can do.

3) Do not offer solutions, advice or encourage the other person list all the things that they can feel positive about in their life. This can make you feel like you are doing something constructive (and make you feel like you are helping) and so can make *you* feel better. However it will probably make the suicidal person feel worse. They want to feel like they are being seen and heard and acknowledged for the pain they are in. Offering solutions, or trying to be positive is a bit like saying "don't feel that!" about how the suicidal person is feeling, which negates their feelings, and means they don't feel heard – and feel even more misunderstood and alone. Besides, if you start to list all the positive things in their life, before they are ready to do so, they will want to punch you in the face.

4) You can however remind them that they matter, and that their feelings matter.

5) Let your loved one be a snot face. You don't need to offer tissues, or a cup of tea. We can often do that to try to feel like we are doing something positive – to help us feel better because we feel like we're helping our loved one. If, however, someone is in the midst of tears, offering a cup of tea or tissues will distract them from the depth of the emotional pain and the experience of releasing their pain – they can then stop crying momentarily, to answer your question. This means they stop releasing those tears, and releasing that pain, as their attention is diverted to thinking about tissues or a cup of tea. Healing happens when we let our emotions out, so don't get in the way of emotions being released – let the emotions flow, and wait until after it's all been released before offering tissues or a cup of tea.

6) If your loved one isn't crying, and is just catatonically still (and quietly in pain), just sit with them. Gently stroke their head, or hold their hand. Every now and then, tell them that you are still here with them. Allow them to be there for a while. It may be an hour or much longer. This is a deep grief or sorrow state they are in. It can take time to come out of it, but it needs to be done gently. A lot of healing can be happening in that stillness that you might not be able to see. There will come a time when you can ask if you can get them a cup of tea, and them having had you just there with them for a while, still and with them, will hopefully help them be able to come out of that state and respond. Professional help may at some point be needed, however being in this deep state of sorrow and pain is the body and mind and soul's way of shutting down to protect itself from any more pain and to heal in some way. I think it would help us to see this positively rather than to fear it. It's important to say that, sometimes, following this state, if the person seems better and has more energy, it doesn't mean they aren't still suicidal – in fact, they may then have the energy to make an attempt. So do find out how they're doing, even after they seem "better".

7) After allowing time for tears, for releasing pain, for healing, by just being with your loved one, there is one question which, I think, is one of the most powerful questions that you can ask, when your loved one is ready to speak. The key is to ask it gently, and kindly – to speak from your heart to theirs.

   "What do you *need*?"

   Often we respond with practical answers, or with an "I don't know". But if we ask the question again, in a deeper, more meaningful and profound way, when someone says "I don't know"......it can open a door to the person releasing even more about how they feel. The truthful answer to this question is often a deep feeling from the heart – I've heard others say things like

"To not be so alone anymore" or
"To be cared about" or
"For someone to bloody hear me"

Or whatever it is.

Again, rather than offering opinions or solutions, listen, reflect what your loved one has said back to them, so that they are prompted to talk more. For example you can say "You don't want to be so alone anymore". Or you can always say "Tell me more (about that)".

When we are given the space to be vulnerable, to be heard and seen, we can heal a lot, and feel better more quickly.

8) Professional help may be necessary. Talk to your loved one about getting more help if you feel out of your depth, or if you feel it is necessary. If you are not sure what to do, you can always call a helpline like The Samaritans or a mental health charity helpline like Lind and ask their advice about how you can best support your loved one. You might also feel it best to call for professional help. Listen to your own inner compass about what you feel is the right thing to do, and do ask for advice from these organisations if you feel out of your depth.

9) There may come a time when your loved one is ready for something to eat or drink. There is clear scientific evidence now proving that most of our serotonin (happy hormone) is made in the gut, so gut health – and the food we eat is absolutely crucial for our mental health.

Make your loved one an organic smoothie of delicious fruits and berries and kale and spinach. Make food that is only organic and so free from pesticides (which carry the energy of death – your loved one needs only foods that bring them the energy of life). On that basis, while they are in this state, only plant food (again carrying the energy of life), rather than meat and dairy (carry the energy of death and sorrow).

Also, a really good bit of vegan organic great quality dark chocolate or cacao or even healthy great quality vegan cake is amazing for the soul. Chocolate is what Professor Lupin always gives to Harry after the Dementors (representing depression) attack in Harry Potter. Cheap crap chocolate, cakes, sweets are terrible for the body, mind or soul – they just makes us feel more sick, destroy gut health, and so suppress our ability to make serotonin – the happy hormone made in our gut. But good quality vegan organic dark chocolate, cacao or healthy vegan free-from cakes literally lift the spirits. It contains theobromine, which is a great mood lifter, and 70% or 95% dark chocolate has been shown to also activate the production of stem cells in the body, and boost the immune system. It has to be vegan – cow's milk inhibits the body's ability to absorb the goodness from the chocolate in the gut.

Some probiotics might help change the microbiome in the gut to a healthier state as well.

As a student homeopath, I have seen some amazing results with the use of homeopathy to change people's states, including suicidal states, and severe depression. I explain the science of it on my website www.danicaapolline.co.uk Maybe arrange for your loved one to see a good practical homeopath, or a naturopath. There are some wonderful medicinal herbs that support mental and physical health too.

These things cost money. If your loved one needs help with getting these due to financial reasons, and you can help, please do so. We can be so private about money, and keep it to ourselves, and sharing it at times like this to help others without easy access to it, who may have no safety net, and giving it freely, is another way we can help in the short term whilst they get back on their feet.

Mental health services

It is a sad fact that, for ordinary people who aren't financially well-off, accessing really good quality support and help needs more thought, funding and input.

I was very, very lucky after my hanging that I had an opportunity to spend 6 weeks as a day patient on a really profound therapeutic programme, run by the NHS at my local hospital. I decided to tell my GP about what I had done, and he was so wonderful. and he arranged a referral to mental health services.

The therapeutic programme wasn't what I was first offered however. I was referred to a psychiatrist. I explained my circumstances, and that I just needed someone to speak to, to help me understand my life, and asked him to refer me to a therapist. He said therapy would only be possible if I agreed to take antidepressants, and that if I refused to take antidepressants (I didn't want them), then he would take it as a sign that I wasn't willing to help myself, and so wouldn't arrange talking therapy.

I still think this was outrageous, and a complete abuse of power. But I wanted therapy, and felt bullied into taking the drugs. Prozac didn't work, so I was put on double the normal dose, which just kept me awake, before I was prescribed some awful mega-brain-death old fashioned tricyclic drug called imipramine, and that's when I just stopped taking the drugs, because I felt so ill – and unlike myself. I felt completely disconnected to myself and my world, and I needed help to be *reconnected.* That's what I was asking for in having access to a talking therapy. I was craving a feeling of being connected to me and my life and to this world in ways that were safe and happy. The drugs were never going to give me that.

But I did get offered a place on the therapeutic programme. It was one of the most profound healing experiences of my life. This of course, due to funding, doesn't exist anymore. But it was life-changing for me. The reason that I talk about it here, is that I feel we need to collectively look at how we can provide safe spaces that are a sanctuary for people who feel so alone and suicidal, that don't require people to be medicated, that are about healing the heart and soul, and nourishing the body and mind too, and that these need to be made available no matter the financial circumstances of people who need them.

We were picked up by taxi every morning (to make sure we got there), and taken to the Unit. We had a daily programme that included group sessions exploring different aspects of childhood, parenting, life, relationships, challenges, how we deal with hard times. We had dramatherapy sessions, art sessions, individual sessions with a psychotherapist, and fun times together too, like going to play bowling. It was profoundly healing. I felt held, safe and cared for, for the first time in my life. I went on to see my psychotherapist from there for 18 months until I graduated, and I still look back on the sessions I had with him and feel like they saved my life.

I was very very lucky. Usually in-patient psychiatric wards really aren't nice places, I know this from having worked as a mental health keyworker. Psychiatric wards are places of medication and containment, not healing and therapy. But this day programme was brilliant.

I personally feel that we need more of this – not drugs – but human care and kindness. And with all we know about health, to create sanctuaries that include gentle yoga sessions, reflexology and massage, healing, the most nourishing organic vegan food it's possible to provide, access to homeopathy and herbalism and naturopathy. And love and kindness and care. A feeling of safety.

I work with people who have no safety net; grown-up orphans on low incomes, single parents, and that is a hard life to live. And then people on low incomes don't get nutrients they need from great quality organic healthy food, their gut microbiome is compromised due to a poor (cheap) diet and the stress of worrying about how they will make ends meet, and we now know from research that this is needed as much for mental health as anything else. Just eating non-organic meat, filled with antibiotics will destroy any gut health – and so negatively affect brain health and our ability to fell happy and resilient.

I hate to admit it, but we do need at least some money to live a healthy lifestyle – more than many people have. We all deserve to feel safe, warm, held, and have all we need to be healthy.

I don't know how this can happen, but it's a dream for me to see places of respite and healing that people can go to and feel held, and heard, and seen, and loved and cared for, and looked after in a healthy way. For everyone to know they have a place of safety somewhere. There is more than enough money in world for every one of us to live a healthy life, my greatest wish is to realise a world where money isn't a barrier for anyone to be healthy, happy and safe, where no-one has a ridiculous amount of money they will never be able to spend, a world where everyone has plenty. We have the money and resources to make this happen, we just need the will (or the revolution!).

Ancient Wisdoms on Birth and Death

I really feel that we have a time to be born and a time to die. Before I talk about death, I would like to explain a few wisdoms about birth, because I think they are linked and related. Before I do, can I just tell you something? As you will have read, I *love* science. I am secretly a bit of a nerd. I used to think that the things I am about to talk about – about spirituality and the soul – were an irrelevance at best. I have come to realise, through my experiences before and since my journey at Platt Fields, that we live in a world of possibilities; that there is a place for science, but there is also a place for ancient traditions and wisdom, and truths can be found in both, and I have learned to have an open mind, that still questions, but that understands that there is more to life than our modern approach science can explain on its own.

Well, actually, science is catching up and proving what ancient wisdoms have taught for Millenia. For example, that we have an electro-magnetic field that extends around our body that we cannot see with our physical eyes. In fact, atoms are actually ONLY 1% physical matter, and 99% space (or energy). We are made of atoms, therefore we can only be 1% physical matter and 99% space (or energy). This is what Einstein taught us: "Everything is energy". Our energy field is HUGE. And is the focus of important research, particularly coming out of the HeartMath Institute in the USA, which has been measuring how far the electromagnetic field of the heart can reach.

I give examples of this in my book *Nature's Medicine Code*, which is a theory about medicine, food and health.

Back to birth, death and suicide.

Older anthroposophical, tribal and ancient religious traditions believe that we are each born at the perfect moment for us, in the perfect way, place and time. At the moment of our birth, as we look directly up at the sky from the place we have been born, there is a map in the stars that describes who we are, the strengths and gifts we bring, some of the challenges we have chosen to face.

In order to be the people who we have chosen to be, we have to be born at a specific time, in a specific location in the world, so that the stars and planets can be mapped with the energies that we will be literally imprinted with, in order to express who we have chosen to be, and to make the differences we have decided to make.

I used to think Astrology was rubbish, and still don't think much about daily horoscopes, but someone explained to me what an astrological birth chart actually was, and this actually made complete sense to me.

Wise and ancient teachers such as the Ancient Greek Pythagoras used to teach Astrology as well as Science, Mathematics, Music, Astronomy – all subjects that were once upon time understood to be related to one another, not separate and distinct, as we have in our world.

An astrological birth chart is this. At the moment we are born, in the place on the Earth we are born, if we look straight up at the sky, the planets and the stars will be mapped in a very specific way. It is a picture unique to that moment, and a baby born at the same time somewhere else in the world will have a different map, unique to them, above them.

I love the work of the hypnotherapist Michael Newton, author of *Life Between Lives* and *Journey of Souls.* He is a hypnotherapist who didn't believe in anything beyond this world, and specialised in helping people stop smoking and losing weight. The thing was, his clients during his sessions kept going to some place that he thought was strange, a place where they were choosing their next life. After over a hundred clients visited this space, reporting exactly the same process of choosing our lives, personalities, bodies and key relationships, he realised he had better start paying attention. They were clearly reporting something significant and meaningful.

This begs the question that, if we choose our lives before we come, why would anyone – any soul – choose to have a painful experience?

Some of the best explanations I have come across I found in the *Conversations with God* series by Neale Donald Walsch. I really recommend these books – this isn't about a Christian or Muslim or any religious "God", these books describe a God that is, in essence, the God of All Things – an energy, I suppose, that we are all said to have come from.

In essence, each of us has a soul. Our soul is a part of "God", a bigger energy. In order that "God" can know itself, it has to see a reflection. Like we only know who we are by the reflection we see in the mirror, or through what we learn about who we are in our relationships, "God" can only know itself through reflections. We are those reflections. That is why the phrase "The God Of All Things" – we are all said to be an expression of God. A different and unique expression of God, but an expression of God nevertheless.

Simply put, our souls choose to have certain experiences, without judging it to be good or bad – just in order that the soul can grow. Our soul will have different experiences in different lifetimes – in this lifetime, my soul chose to have this experience, but in another lifetime, I could have had a blissfully happy childhood. Maybe even with the same souls as my Mum and Dad, but in those lifetimes, they may have chosen to be balanced, happy people so that my childhood was happy.

In order for our souls to grow, we choose to experience and learn different things. I was shown that I chose to learn wisdom, and in order to do that, I have chosen to go through many different experiences to help me develop it.

I may not have been able to consciously choose – once I was born – what all of my experiences were, because these I had already decided. But we are able to make choices, and my choice has been to learn and to grow as much as I can, to heal the pain, and to share what I have learned to help others with their challenges. I could have chosen not to do that as well, but my personality and who I am in this life mean I was Born Feisty – that I have a tenacity that applies itself to how I learn, heal and make a difference to others as well. I champion making the world a better place. My experiences have helped me to want to do that. That is why I chose pain, so I could help others transform theirs. But I see pain not just at an individual level, I see pain caused by structures and models we see in business, societies, economies, politics, governance and in humanity. I have lived these too.

I really believe that you will have chosen your own relationships, challenges, gifts before you came, but the choices we have are *how we respond* to what life throws at us. If we are powerful, we make powerful choices in how we respond. If we don't believe we are powerful, then we won't make powerful choices. I love witnessing people realise that they *are* powerful, when they didn't believe that they were.

There is another way of looking at all of this – the why we have challenges, and how they help us. It is described by a model called *The Hero's Journey.*

The Hero's Journey

Each and every individual story, be it your story, or a story in a book or film, can be described as following the same pattern.

Joseph Campbell was a Professor of Literature who was fascinated by mythology. He studied the myths of many cultures and religions and those of historical interest. He explored Native American, Aboriginal, Hindu and Ancient Greek mythologies and even stories from the Bible and the legends of King Arthur.

He identified that every myth and every story has, in essence, the same tale told within it. He called this "The Hero's Journey" or "The Universal Story".

The Hero's Journey represents the journey through life, and has three parts to it: Separation, Initiation and Return.

During Separation, we are in one experience of life. We don't know any differently, so we just live it. We live according to limitations (listening to "shoulds"), and not expressing our highest and greatest potential fully. The highest vision of ourselves is completely hidden to us, and we have no idea of what we are fully capable of. We build around us a world of limitation that keeps us "In our place" – the media, consumerism, instant gratification all serve to keep us in a trance of how we should be living.

Then something happens that shakes us out of this sleepwalk through life. The Initiation can be triggered by a challenging situation. It is a call to awaken, and if we don't respond to the initial callings, then what comes will be very challenging – so big we just can't ignore it. It may be the death of someone, or a painful divorce or sudden illness, or losing a job. Our life gets turned upside down in some way, and during this awakening we have no idea of what we will be doing eventually, once we have come through our journey.

Often there are aspects of the Initiation that are so wonderful – seeing the world in a whole new way – seeing the wonder and magic in life. But it is a journey to realising your awesomeness and so there have to be challenges too.

The Initiation is an invitation to realize that you are a Hero, a person of greatness, but in order to realize this, we go through a time of having to overcome many obstacles where ultimately we face the greatest fears we can imagine. Initiation is a call to adventure, and we start to see that there is a greater version of ourselves – it is our true self. Often the people around us don't want us to go down the path that leads us to explore new ways of experiencing ourselves and the world around us. We start to work through our limitations as a way of breaking through them. We eventually reach the point where we are ready to take on our greatest fears and limitations that have formed into some kind of mythical monster. Campbell described how we have to take on our "dragons", as he called them – and slay them. We go through massive transformation and a death of all that we no longer need.

Once we have completed the challenges we have faced, we Return to share our story of what we have overcome and then help others to find their own way through their personal experience of The Hero's Journey.

The way to slay the dragon is to stop fighting it, and then *love* your dragon. Your dragon holds a gift for you – maybe an awareness of your strengths, a leap to being free from limitations, and so realising your potential in your life, and doing brilliantly, or it may be a realization that the dragon is a part of you, and that you are beautiful with it.

In essence, the Initiation, the slaying our dragons – learning to love our greatest fears – is beautifully represented by Luke Skywalker going to the Dagobah System and facing an imaginary Darth Vader in the swamp in Empire Strikes Back. The Hobbit, Lord of The Rings, Harry Potter all have a similar invitation for the hero to face their greatest fears in order to accomplish something amazing.

I also think The Truman Show is an amazing representation of this. In the beginning, Truman Brubaker has no idea his life is actually a TV set. He happily bumbles along. But then he awakes. He realizes that his life isn't actually how he thought it was. He wants to leave and learn about the world (grow), but every time he thinks of leaving, huge warnings of plane crashes and ships sinking pop up to stop him making the leap and going out into the world. He learns he has to trust himself, and his instincts, and to have courage and go for his dreams. Eventually he has to face the weather disaster created by the TV show maker, and face his greatest fears – that he will die – and eventually he comes though and out the other side, to freedom. We of course never get to see his "Return", but this film is a great depiction of the first two parts of the Hero's Journey.

So in those moments when life feels hard, it may also help to remember that maybe you are in the Dagobah System of your life; in the Initiation when you are invited to overcome your greatest fears and challenges, and find your courage and strength and resilience in the process. And that if you keep walking forward, you may have a story to share as part of your Return.

There is a beautiful film called *Finding Joe,* which describes Campbell's Hero's Journey with inspiring and illuminating examples of people who have made it through the Initiation. The shows how so many of the films that we look to that inspire us all have the same story. The Lord of the Rings, The Hobbit, Star Wars, E.T, Harry Potter to name a few all are examples of that one story of life, the same story that applies to yours – The Hero's Journey.

Our choice to die

So ancient wisdoms teach that there is a time in which our soul is born, to have the experiences it wants to have, with the people it chooses to experience them with.

And the same is said to be true of how we die too. Our souls are said to choose when to die, in which way, to give us and others an experience that our soul chooses to have. I can see how my Mum died at the perfect time for her, in the perfect way, even though she was only 47 years old. It absolutely was her time, I know that, however much I would love for her to have lived longer. Her soul wanted to leave. She literally died at the ending of a Millenium during Millenium New Year's Eve. So many people tell amazing stories about how their loved ones should have died earlier, but waited until all their loved ones were gathered at their bedside (or, as in my Mum's case, the moment everyone had left her room, despite someone being with her in every moment apart from 1 crucial minute – she wanted to die on her own).

It's hard sometimes to look at how people can die in horrible ways, and believe that people really might have *chosen* to experience that. But I always think that there are so many ways in which good things come out of "bad". I don't follow the news very much, but when my son happens to hear anything on the radio, I always say to him "For every one horrible bit of news, know that there are MILLIONS of people RIGHT NOW doing wonderful things for other people. It's just that you won't hear it on the news."

When sad, or tragic, or horrible things happen, there is always a powerful rising of goodness, or love, of kindness. Of people helping. We only, as I have already shared, see the Light because the darkness exists, and the darkness is the call for the Light to shine more brightly.

If we choose our experiences, does it mean that we should leave people to have their experiences and not step in to help?

I have occasionally heard some spiritual people suggest that it is best to allow people to go through their challenges, and not intervene, as this is what they chose, as this is what their soul chose to experience.

This is a bit like being a parent. It's really hard to watch our little ones go through challenges – we want to save them from any pain at all. But it IS how we grow, and get stronger, and learn resilience.
However there ARE times when we MUST step in, and we have to listen to when we have to step back and allow people the right to make their own choices, and when to step forward and intervene.

For example, in cases of abuse. I have heard the odd spiritual teacher say "well, they chose that experience" as a reason not to step in and help. Fortunately it's a very rare opinion, but it's important to name it for what it is - spiritual bullshit.

If someone needs help - is being abused, or treated badly, particularly in the case of children, or in any case where there is an abuse of power, for people of any age, I believe it is our *duty* to take action and step in to help. We must never ever ignore people in those circumstances who need our help.

So back to talking about suicide.

If we are born as we are meant to be born, and die as we are meant to die, can this include suicide?

My experience suggests that yes, it can include suicide. Because I wasn't allowed through. But other people are.

Choosing suicide not an easy choice. It's not, as has historically been claimed, a cowards choice. It's hard to go against Darwin's evolutionary desire to survive. It requires a total disconnection emotionally from all those we love and care for in order to carry it out.

People can think we must feel desperate when trying to end our lives, but that wasn't my experience. Desperation can come from living, but there can be a strange yet remarkable peacefulness in dying.

Yet at the same time as that, I have lived through bereavement, and lived the grief process that followed my Mum dying, and I also know how painful it can be to have someone we love die.

In many ways, once a person takes their own life, they may be in a wonderful place, but the loved ones that remain then have to deal with the pain of losing someone – and sometimes the guilt of wondering if there is any more that they could have done.

Keith Flint from The Prodigy's death has had me reflect a lot on this. Actually it's because of his suicide that I have come to share what I have shared here, this book exists because he died. I realised my story was helping some people understand that he chose his time, and was encouraged to tell my story more widely, so that it hopefully helps more people.

It's hard to imagine anything good coming out of his death. However, something really important is happening because he died.

Rave culture is going through a massive resurgence, with tribute raves to Keith Flint popping up all around the world. DJs are paying tribute in their sets. Goodness knows what Ibiza will be like this summer, and Glastonbury Festival, where The Prodigy had been due to perform, will probably see Out of Space and Firestarter played a million times.

The Warriors, as Prodigy fans are called, are rising. Connecting. Sharing. Remembering. And raving once more. We are tuning back into that amazing vibe that made us into a tribe – a family. One family. One love.

What Keith's passing has done is to reunite people who were part of that near-revolution. Who remember that shift in consciousness. Who remember what it meant to see a broken system; corrupt, uncaring, political structures designed to save the few and break the many. Who wanted to break free from the 1980s Thatcherite self-serving ideologies, and remember that none of us is an island, that we are all here together, as one family, and need love as the glue that binds us.

The timing of this is almost poetic to me. I look at people YEARNING for togetherness, completely revulsed by political structures and figures and policies that don't care about the people they are supposed to represent. With so much political instability, Brexit and climate change, people are agitating for change. Huge change. We have had enough.

I am always reminded of what I have seen, on the 2 occasions I have seen people collapse on the London Underground, during busy rush hour times. The people immediately around the collapsing commuter stepped forward to hold them; to help them. No-one looked at their watch thinking "I'm going to be late for work". They cared for their fellow human being, and prioritised a stranger's needs over their own. This is, I think, our natural way of being. We allow fears to get in the way, but our innate instinct knows we need each other to survive. We need each other to thrive.

Love is rising. We are connecting. From the incredible Greta Thunberg and the children taking part in the climate protests, to the rapidly growing Extinction Rebellion, to those of us who can see the damage being done by 5G, Big Pharma and Biotech companies, to those of us waiting.......just waiting for the next elections......we are RISING.

We are Remembering we are One, that we have to look after one another, that love is all that matters. We are remembering how music and art can be used to bring people together; that life, people and our world is amazing. This is happening for us older ravers because Keith died, joined by a whole new generation of younger people who can see what we see, a need to break out of a system that doesn't work and just dance, rebel, be together, love.

He left us some gifts in his passing. I get the feeling his work here isn't done – that he is now helping us all to reconnect and rise in ways that wouldn't have happened had he continued to live.

People are talking more about suicide and mental health, asking each other to reach out and ask for help if they need it. People are being more caring of one another.

He achieved so much in his life, and now is achieving so much in his death too. He was allowed to pass through – it was his time.

Whereas for me, I still had work to do here on the Earth. I still had a difference to make, so I wasn't allowed through. I really believe that if you are here, like me, you still have a difference to make too.

The ultimate cause of depression and sadness – and the way to fix it, and our world?

As I have mentioned, I am now studying to be a homeopath. The shifts I have seen in other people's health and my own *astound* me. There is so much research, being collated by the Homeopathy Research Institute, despite what pharmaceutical companies and some scientists would have you believe (and remember I say this as someone whose whole life was going to be about Pharmacy!).

In 1862, Abraham Lincoln signed a bill allocating some civil war military hospitals over to homeopaths because of their unparalleled success in treating cholera, yellow fever, diptheria and influenza compared to conventional medicine. During a 2007 epidemic of leptospirosis in Cuba, a homeopathic medicine was given to 2.3 million people at high risk of infection, while the remaining 8.8 million population were left untreated. The total number of infections in the treated area dropped from 401 cases in 2007 to 64 in 2008 representing a 84% decline in incidence, whereas the non-treated area saw an increase in number of cases from 309 cases in 2007 to 376 in 2008 representing a 21% increase. There was no placebo control for this, so it isn't a clinical trial, however these results are astounding. And to me now, understanding what I understand about health and homeopathy, which I explain in *Nature's Medicine Code*, This Is Not A Surprise.

The reason I mention homeopathy is this.

The German medical doctor, Dr Samuel Hahnemann who discovered homeopathy wrote, in the philosophy behind it, about the cause of all disease – mental, emotional, physical and spiritual.

He described how there are 4 aspects to a whole person:

- The body
- The mind
- The soul (this is where we just are who we are)
- The spirit (this is out connection to Source / some higher spiritual aspect). In essence this is our connection to God (meant in a non-religious, spiritual way).

Dr Hahnemann said that all dis-ease is caused by the disquiet that happens when the mind does something that isn't aligned with the spirit (God).

In other words, our highest aspect knows what is wonderful for us and what isn't. it knows when we do wonderful things for another, and when we don't. And when we don't, even when our mind tries to justify it, some inner subconscious part of us knows and *feels* uncomfortable, feels out of integrity. That disquiet; that *dissonance* as psychologists would describe it, creates the perfect conditions for disease to set in.

As one of my tutors explained, it's like this. Imagine you are driving down a beautiful country road, and enjoying the trees and view, whilst drinking a take-away cup of coffee. Your mind says "right! I've finished that cup of coffee.", and you throw the cup out of the window. Your mind will say "Oh, it doesn't matter, it's only a cup". But your Spirit *knows* that wasn't the right thing to do, it *knows* we must look after our planet, it *knows* that wasn't a kind thing to do. That forms a *gap* between the Mind and the Spirit, and that GAP is where disease sets in.

So, to close the gap, we must listen to our highest aspect, we must listen to what love would do. Integrity means wholeness means listening to our highest wisdom means health.

This applies not just to us individually, but to our decisions in business, to how research is conducted in science, to how foods are genetically modified (or not), to how we treat homeless people, to how we work together as colleagues, to how we educate our children and look after our sick, and world and planet.

This isn't, by the way, about going back to some archaic view of how we live our lives. I don't want any pro-lifers to get excited about this "listen to Spirit / your highest knowing about the right thing to do / God" section, and think I think it applies to abortions too, because I don't. It's about asking the question "what is the kindest thing to do, for everyone, and the planet, taking all of the factors into consideration?" Abortion may be the kindest choice – maybe for a pregnant woman overwhelmed by how much she is already juggling, who would find it hard to cope, or just doesn't feel ready, or doesn't want to have a child full stop, and so maybe that is the kindest choice for the unborn child too.

We KNOW that it isn't right that people sleep on the streets, that people work hard but still live in poverty because of low incomes, that junior doctors, teachers, nurses, firefighters are paid badly yet some people earn millions every year. We KNOW that it's not OK that our clothes are made in sweatshops. We KNOW that it's not OK that trees have been chopped down for logging, or for 5G, or for whatever reasons. We KNOW it's not OK for Nestle and Coca-Cola and other companies to take precious clean water supplies that belong indigenous tribes and sell it to us all. But we live in a world where we still buy cheap clothes, and cheap food, and eat McDonalds and drink Coco-cola. We KNOW it isn't right to test anything or animals. We KNOW it's disgusting to use aborted foetal tissue for ANY reason (which they are – for vaccines and stem cell therapy). We KNOW it's wrong to make human medicines in the bodies of live animals (again, some vaccines). We KNOW it's not right that people are treated differently because of the colour of their skin. There's the gap. So our world is full of dis-eased behaviour and conditions that most of us (all of us who aren't unfeeling psychopaths) know is wrong (and that we can ensure changes).

Organic farming? Done kindly? We would hope so. Natural products made only with nature's oils and plants? That's kindness right there. Meat factories? A hothouse of unkindness. Petrochemicals companies making products with synthetic chemicals that cause cancer and hormone problems – and who KNOW this is the case – as well as people who knowing this make money selling them, whilst knowingly polluting rivers and the planet? Yet more unkindness right there. And us *buying* these foods and products, knowing they cause harm? That's the gap right there. That's what we can change – and *are changing*. You and me and all of us.

This is about looking at everything, all the factors in any decision – personal, professional, shopping, planetary. And choosing the kindest solution taking all those factors into consideration.

We are seeing a dis-eased planet because we have allowed our minds to stop caring. We see dis-eased people because we have disconnected from loving one another. We can change that, we ARE changing that. With every decision we make, we can choose to be aligned to love and kindness or to not caring. More and more of us are choosing love. More and more of us are being the change.

That ultimately is what makes us as people healthy, and our world healthy.

Think you can't do it? Think you are too small to make a difference? As the Dalai Lama so eloquently says, "if you think you are too small to make a difference, spend the night with a mosquito".

And also look to vegans. Vegans are changing the world, one by one by changing their eating and shopping habits. Restaurants have vegan menus now, supermarkets whole sections dedicated to vegans.

A reflection on suicide and money

There is one aspect of our world and life on it – a dis-ease that I would like to talk about.

The only times (other than one) that I felt suicidal since my time in Platt Fields have been because of huge challenges financially.

Part of my journey has included experiencing what it is like to live without a stable income, or a proper living wage, despite working really hard.

There have been times, despite working really hard, I have had nothing in the bank, and no way of knowing how I would next be able to buy food, rent, put money on the gas meter or pay for my travel to get to work.

I had done a lot of work on clearing blocks and barriers, a **huge** amount. I had seen myself as an abundant person for a long, long time. I feel abundant in my heart. I am surrounded by goodness.

There have been times when, despite working very hard, and being paid well for the sectors I have worked in, but still, like junior doctors and nurses and teachers, I have received benefits to top up my income.

Benefits. I am grateful to have received all I have. But my goodness, what we expect people to survive on - and stay health and well - is farcical. People talk about benefits cheats, but the people I know who supplement their income, but are busy making the world a better place are really not benefit cheats.

Have I fucked up some monetary decisions in my life? Oh royally yes! Have I stuck my head in the sand and not dealt with difficult money decisions because the anxiety and panic has been so great that I couldn't breathe let alone think about how to move forward? Absolutely I have!

But there have been times I have gone through my finances with a fine tooth comb, and realised - accepted - that I genuinely couldn't tell myself I have been crap with money, or that I am wrong. Or that I was in "poverty consciousness".

Which is what you are expected to think of yourself if you have zero in the bank.

J.K.Rowling was not in "poverty consciousness" when she was writing Harry Potter. Her creativity didn't come from desperation to be rich, it came from an inner call that she heard and responded to that was about sharing something amazing. Her abundant soul enabled her to create something life-changing for so many people whilst her financial circumstances were difficult.

The same is true of life before fame for actors, and musicians and gurus.

Creatives who haven't yet "made it" are not necessarily in poverty consciousness - that is just spiritual bullshit. We live in a world that doesn't honour and respect creativity.

How do I know? Every time I see a busker, I always stop and give money as a thank you for making me smile. And then I watch the countless people who walk by giving nothing. And, to be honest, it really upsets me. If a busker has made you smile, please give them some money as a thank you! Honour them for sharing their remarkable talent with you. It takes a lot of courage to be out in a public place singing, it's the least we can do for the happiness they make us feel.

We need to change how we see creativity. We NEED it to feel connected. The feelings evoked by books we read, the art we see, the amazing photographs of smiles, friendship, animals and nature we see, music that stirs our soul, films that inspire us.

And the healers and natural medicine women and men connecting us with our health. Doctors and nurses saving us in times of emergency. Our teachers who inspire us.

Surviving on little money, despite hard work is punishingly hard, and 100% totally, completely unnecessary in our world. There is more than enough for everyone to live comfortably. The stress of trying to cope financially with little – and stay well and healthy – isn't acceptable in my world, and is another sign of a dis-eased world. And the reason for that is this.

Money is one of the big elephants in the room. A silent shadow, that people don't speak about. Whether rich or poor, people don't talk about how much money they have, how they spend it – this is seen as "private", so it goes into shadow. And becomes unspoken along with the guilt, shame, fear and misery people can feel.

The saying "money can't buy you happiness" is true to a point – but living with less than we need to live comfortably – seriously struggling can make us miserable, and that's not fair in our abundant world.

In every trial of a proper living income, crime levels drop, drug use drops, and people end up working more, doing what they love, starting their own businesses.

THIS is what a healthy world does.

So we need to stop the shame people have around money. Some people have it, some people don't - but it is NOT a reflection of how much anyone matters, or how much of a positive influencer, or a success they are.

.

We keep money issues hidden, and because they are hidden, they aren't addressed properly within the collective. We have made money a reason for separation and we can make it about togetherness, but first we need to learn how to talk about it openly, without judgement, without fear, shame or guilt.

It's time we change the nature of the conversation.

There is a suggestion in one of Neale Donald Walsch's *Conversations With God* books. It is that people selling products gave more information: not only the price of the product or service, but also how much it costs to produce it, and therefore how much profit is being made? I think this would be amazing, and stop ridiculous amounts of greed. And I would suggest adding how much the actual producer / maker received out of all that money would be great too.

I know people with little money who are embarrassed about how little they have and wealthy people embarrassed about how much they have, and this inequality – this imbalance would only cease to exist if we all knew how much we all earned, and how much we had.

Money isn't the problem. Money can be used for so much good in the world. I look forward to buying up rainforests one day. It is *how we use it* and how we have made it a secret, that the secret has become a shadow and is eating away at us all in some way shape or form.

The utter terror of not knowing if you have enough to survive, or to feed your family is a horrendous and totally unnecessary pressure in our world and this can lead to people feeling suicidal – and to choosing to end their lives. It's a horrible way to have to live, and I know what it is like to do everything in your power to be financially stable but it not be easy. This is something we can change, by all being transparent, open, and calling in transparency from others, and demanding equality, abundance, and a healthy baseline income for all.

A little message to those serving humanity but barely making ends meet - if you are listening to the call of how you can best help humanity and serve love, you are NOT in poverty consciousness, you are NOT a failure, or less worthy than others if your bank account isn't filled with tons of money. You are in creative service. So keep going. Just keep going.

Think it's too hard to change our world? That there is too much that needs to be done? That it's too late. Think again.

This is one of my favourite examples of how it's never too late, and how miracles really can and do happen.

There is always hope

One of my favourite examples of how it's never too late, and how miracles really can and do happen, comes from World War Two.

It is what happened on Dunkirk beach, in France, told beautifully in Christopher Nolan's film *Dunkirk.*

In 1940, almost all of the British army – around 380,000 British soldiers - were on Dunkirk beach, and were surrounded by Nazi troops who were moving towards the beach from all sides. It looked like they would all be killed, and in fact, the British Government were preparing to lose most of their soldiers. They were expecting to lose 90% of their soldiers, and it looked like the War would be lost to the Nazis. It looked like it was an impossible situation. But a miracle happened.

At the very last moment, ordinary fishermen from England took their small fishing boats, and crossed the channel, and rescued the British soldiers, in small numbers, going back and forth across the channel. Instead of losing 90% of the Army, 300,000 of the 380,000 soldiers were rescued. It literally was a miracle.

I think it's a really important thing to remember. It always looks like the darkness will win, there is a moment when everyone gives up. In that moment of surrender, when we stop fighting miracles *can* happen, like happened at Dunkirk.

Midwives and obstetricians know that a baby is always about to be born when the mother says "Right! That's it! I am not doing this anymore. I want this to stop now". It tickles me that an old friend actually told her partner to pack her things, that she'd had enough and they were leaving and going home now. Her son was born a few minutes later.

It is when life feels most bleak that things change. Following my paracetamol overdose, and following my hanging, life really did change for the better and quickly.

The one constant in life is change. Nothing ever stays the same. If we can hold on through the tough times, there are always lighter times ahead.

I think this is really relevant to us now, in our world, and in our times, with climate change, and political corruption, corporate greed......there is a saying that the night is always darkest before the dawn, and I think that is where we are at now in the world. We are seeing the worst, but we are rising and saying it's enough too. Love is driving out hate, and changing our world for the better. We only have to look at the Greta Thunbergs.....the children of our world, standing up and speaking up, and we can see our world is in safe hands.

My one issue with all of the fear and anxiety about Brexit and the Climate that I see, is that we are losing sight of good things being possible. We might not be able to plan and see what lies ahead, but I think we could really help ourselves by believing that good outcomes *are* possible, even if we can't see what they might be right now.

We are focused on what science tells us is and isn't possible, but we have to remember that greater possibilities can occur even beyond what scientists can measure, or believe could happen. Miracles really do happen every day in the world. People, who have been told that they will never get over their cancer, who miraculously do, people told they have a life-long condition such a diabetes, who then find a way to cure it, I have literally seen bones rearrange themselves in a healing session to where they needed to be. I talk about this in more detail, with examples in *Nature's Medicine Code.*

So, whilst it is important to listen to what scientists and experts have to share, I also think we need to have a bigger vision – that no matter what the data might predict – that we must not allow our thinking to be limited by data, or fear – that miraculous outcomes ARE possible, even if we can't see, or imagine, or know how they might happen.

There is a wonderful Chinese proverb that states "The person who says something is impossible should not interrupt the person doing it".

Athletes defy the "impossible" in every Olympics, showing the body is capable of more than we ever thought possible. It was thought that flying would be impossible. Until we did it. It was thought that doing a 360 degree loop on a skateboard without falling off would be impossible. Until someone did it. Eddie the Eagle and the Jamaican Bobsled team and the Paralympians we see are some of the most inspirational athletes, because they have all been told that what they were doing is impossible, and did what they set out to do anyway – to become Olympians. Rosa Parks and Martin Luther King and Nelson Mandela would all have been taught that black people would never live in a world free from enforced segregation. Whilst we see so much racism still today that needs addressing, each of these remarkable great souls saw positive changes in their lifetimes. Gandhi would have been told that overthrowing the British Empire was impossible. But he managed that. History is filled with the impossible being made possible – space flight, speaking to someone on the other side of the world, SEEING them as we speak to them, the list is endless.

It's OK if we don't know what or how a positive outcome might happen. It's OK to say "I don't know how we're going to fix this, or make this better, but we will find a way – there HAS to be a way", and just sit with that question for a few hours, or a few days or a few weeks, or a few months, and see what answers and ideas come to you.

There is *always* another way, *always* another choice we can make, even if we feel powerless, or helpless, or exhausted. In those moments, ask yourself what the ONE next step you can take is. Just take ONE step. Whether it's getting out of bed to brush your teeth, or going to a demonstration, or writing something on social media, just do ONE thing, and it opens the door to you doing more.

Having a sense of purpose

I really believe that we all have a purpose. Some people would say that it is enough that our purpose is that our soul is experiencing life.

I would say that – given where our world is at – that we also have a bigger purpose at this time.

I think we are here to make a difference. To stand up, speak up, reclaim our world as a place where love governs everything from politics to economics, to relationships, to how we treat our planet and all of life on her. Just by talking about what we see and feel with friends and family – even if they disagree with us – is making a difference, sending out a ripple effect through the world.

Marianne Williamson, in her book *The Law of Divine Compensation* talks about how when we are looking for ways to make money, we ask the question "what do I need to do in my career?" or "What job shall I get?".

She advises changing the question to "How can I best *serve?*" which I have found to be a much more powerful question, that really gives us a sense of purpose. It's this question, following Keith Flint's death that has led to me writing this book. I don't know what will happen once I publish it, and I have taken quite a few gulps, as I have shared a lot of really uncomfortable aspects of my life, this is one of the hardest things I have done to share these so publicly. Answering the question "How can I best *serve*?" may call on you to have courage, but courage is what our world needs right now to thrive.

One quote (author unknown) is that "The world suffers a lot. Not because of the violence of bad people, but because of the silence of good people".

Abraham Lincoln, who abolished slavery, said "To sin by silence when they should protest makes cowards of men."

As well as just living, and being in this world, I really believe our greatest purpose is to find our courage. To lovingly challenge people, loved ones, colleagues, bosses, businesses, politicians, about what we see happening that has caused destruction. Love is not a passive force, love can be fiery, passionate, angry, can stand up for what is good in the world.

Love can be feisty

I believe that it wasn't just me who was Born Feisty. I believe we have been born at a time when we all need to be feisty, in our own ways.

So if you have got to the end of this book, know you matter, you are amazing, that there is a difference only you can make, but to make it you need to rise. Do your best each day, live with kindness, and stand up for love. You are here, alive, breathing, beating with a pulse that drives you to live and be the greatest you can be.

I believe in your ability to do it. Even in those times when you don't. I know you can. That's why you and me are here.

Practical steps you can take to make a difference

There are many many practical (and awesome) steps that you can take to play your part in making the world a better place. There are also some really useful health-related tips in *Nature's Medicine Code.*

1) Smile at people and say hello, especially those who need one the most; homeless people, exhausted parents whose children are having a meltdown on the bus, people having a bad day. We all have bad days sometimes, when actually we need to hear someone say "you alright mate?". Be the person who says that to friends and strangers alike.

2) Think about how you can do a Random Act of Kindness for someone else. Some people I know write random love letters and leave them for others to find, to cheer up their day. To read about some great Random Acts of Kindness, read *Join Me* by Danny Wallace. It's really funny and brilliant.

   I once overheard on a bus a conversation a lady was having on the phone to a friend. She was describing how her boyfriend treated her, which I appreciate was only her side of the story, but it didn't sound like she was being cherished. So I wrote her an anonymous note, just telling her that she is beautiful, that she matters, that she deserves to be cherished and treated beautifully always, and then left the note so she would find it as I got off the bus.

   It costs nothing to be spread love.

3) Work on yourself, and heal your pain. This is hard work at times. But when we don't do that, our subconscious pain becomes mirrored and reflected – projected – into the outside world. Drinking and taking drugs and self-medicating only slows that process down. You can walk through your pain, however hard it may seem, and there are people around who can help you. Every time I have spent a concentrated period of

time healing my pain (eg on 3 day healing retreats), I have seen a positive change not just in my life, but in the outside world too.

4) Use your money in ways that Buy The Change – use your money to literally be a vote for love in our world.

   More and more people are changing the world by how they spend their money, the explosion in organic food and more natural products and veganism is another testament to that.

   So what you do with your money – with every single penny of it – can make our world *amazing*. Here are some ideas for how you can use your money with love in our world.

   a) Move ALL your money to only ethical banks. Triodos is the most ethical bank in the UK, or the Co-operative Bank is another, but Triodos is by far the best. Conventional banks invest your money in the arms trade, and make money from fossil fuels and war. You can change that, and put your money with banks that behave differently.

   b) Only buy organic GMO free food. Pesticides and herbicides kill bees, and insects crucial to the ecosystem, and so destroy the growth of new plants and healthy food, as well as causing us cancer, so to have healthy food, it needs to be chemical free, grown as nature intended. You can find out more in *Nature's Medicine Code.*

c) Reduce your meat and dairy intake (and if you can go vegan!) to stop the logging of rainforests – precious trees we need – to create more land for cattle farming.

d) Stop buying processed food, so much of which contains palm oil, which has contributed to some destruction of precious rainforest, and the habitats of orang-utans and other precious wildlife. Love nature, love the animals, love the orang-utans. Learn to cook (or get a partner who can!) and so palm oil won't be needed for food anymore.

e) Buy clothes ethically, using organic cotton where possible, and shop in charity shops. Hemp is a phenomenal material, grows 5x more rapidly than cotton, is naturally anti-bacterial and anti-fungal, is naturally waterproof, and bugs can't stand it, so it never needs pesticides. It's a miracle plant that can be used to make paper (instead of trees!), ropes, tents, clothing, so much of what we need in our world. The more we buy hemp products, the greater the demand will be, and the more companies will turn to using hemp instead of other less effective and more damaging alternatives that we have been using.

f) Buy only 100% natural cleaning products, toiletries, make-up and perfumes. Most toiletries, cleaning products, perfumes and make-up contain synthetic chemicals that disrupt hormones, can cause migraines, can trigger asthma and can even be carcinogenic. Definitely only use 100% natural suncreams – some studies show that skin cancers are actually linked to the use of suncreams.

g) Change how you manage your health. There are fantastic natural approaches to health, including using safe and effective medicinal herbs, homeopathy and nutrition. If you have a chronic health condition, go and see a qualified practical homeopath, medical herbalist, nutritionist or naturopath and find more natural ways to support your health.

There is a wealth of information in *Nature's Medicine Code*, so I am sharing only a snippet here.

h) Buy an electric car if you can afford one. Fossil fuels are the reason for many of the wars and much of the suffering we see in the world, as well as polluting the air we breathe. This way you are moving your money away from wars and towards greater peace in the world, as well as helping clear up the air and reducing the number of children who develop asthma. Electric cars are still not perfect because of how the batteries are manufactured, but this will change, and STILL it beats the use of fossil fuels.

i) Get involved with Citizens Assemblies. These are a truly democratic approach to decision-making, and not like how politics is done at the moment. Currently we live in a corporatocracy where corporations tell a significant number of politicians how to govern, rather than those politicians listening to the citizens who elected them. Citizens Assemblies work in a similar way to jury in some ways - an assembly of ordinary randomly selected people, representative of the whole population demographically, ideally of 100 people, to whom experts present all findings, debate the issues at hand, and EVERYONE, the public can contribute and speak for 2 minutes to suggest ideas for how to move forward. There are clear guidelines around respectful behaviour, decisions are made quickly and easily, and it takes out politicians making decisions, many of whom are on corporate payrolls and are former corporate lobbyists anyway.

It is a citizens assembly that ensured abortion laws in Ireland were finally changed, in Iceland, the whole Government was sacked and it is a country now run by Citizens Assemblies. In Frome, Somerset, England, the Citizens Assembly has been so effective, that it has taken over the running of local services.

j) Shop in ways that love the planet. Zero-waste refills, heat-exchange heating systems, electricity powered 100% by non-nuclear renewable energy, getting your own solar panels, whatever works for you and your budget. Cycle more, walk more, get the bus more.

k) Research 5G, as it's different to 3G and 4G, and talk to other people about it so that we have greater awareness. **It is the single greatest threat to health and to life we have in our world right now – it is an even greater and more immediate threat than climate change.** 4G uses 2.4Ghz, 5G uses 60GHz (and can go up to 300Ghz – up to 125 TIMES the current

EMF radiation levels). It uses microwave energy, and we know from research that microwaves denature blood cells (in other words change their structure and make them useless).

238 EMF Specialist Scientists from 41 countries have made an appeal to the United Nations , World Health Organisation, EU and individual Governments to address the risks posed by EMF radiation, especially to children and foetal development, and stop 5G development on the Earth and in Space.

The science they list is compelling, and at the time of writing, over 93,000 people including leading doctors, scientists and environmentalists have signed the appeal (www.5gspaceappeal.org) Many studies show damage to DNA and disruption of the Blood Brain Barrier (BBB) at levels hundreds of times lower than US exposure limits (www.ehtrust.org). Doctors have been making their own appeal against EMF radiation because of the serious health problems that they are seeing (https://ssita.org.uk/wp-content/uploads/2014/03/British-Doctors-Letter-March-2014.pdf?fbclid=IwAR3nQDIVHrV5SbkgGQUURYln7DtYRBrHqZsrF7QFr9cZy-64R7Ul-xyYBEw)

Early indications with 5G show increased rates of cancer in test areas, including one school in Ripon, California, where 4 children and 3 teachers developed cancers. 5G and smart meters have also been shown to destroy the quality of red blood cells, and decimate the numbers of them (videos available online) – so 5G is dangerous for pregnant women, babies and children. Birds and bees and small animals are being found also to die easily at these high radiation levels.

So don't get a 5G router, and configure your laptop and router to only receive a 2.4GHz signal, not a 5GHz signal (and switch your router off at night always). Think about moving to a non-smart phone or landline – and definitely don't get your kids a smartphone, or buy effective EMF blocking protection, such as that produced by Memon for your devices.

Hardwire your laptop and use an ethernet cable. Sleep on a grounding sheet, and spend time every day that you can standing barefeet on the ground (soil or grass) – this helps to discharge EMF radiation and stress. Cover Smart meters with Faraday covers.

Buy some orgonite or good quality reputable shungite, which you can wear as a pendant or bracelet, to help protect you from excessive EMF radiation. Put a piece of each next to your router. Cleanse these regularly.

And as I said talk to people about it, spread awareness so people have choices. Get together in your local communities and take legal action. 5G frequencies are an assault on the body and, as was successfully proved in a Court in Sydney found, causes injury to the body that can be classed as assault. A street of doctors and lawyers in Sydney had their 5G masts removed because of this case.

There are things we can do about 5G and all of the other issues in our world, especially when we are aware, we just all need to be willing to take action – positive action – rather than to ignore it.

l) Also, 5G and many other policies we face are a challenge to the health and wellbeing of us all, and so go against the **Universal Declaration of Human Rights**.

Article 30 of the Universal Declaration of Human Rights states that "Nothing in this **Declaration** may be interpreted as implying for any State, group or person any **right** to engage in any activity or to perform any act aimed at the destruction of any of the **rights** and freedoms set forth herein". What that means is that no Government has the right to do anything that overrides the rights laid out in the Universal Declaration of Human Rights, including our right to health. Our right to health requires a healthy planet.

I think part of our being feisty is a requirement that we ensure that the Universal Declaration of Human Rights is enacted in full throughout the world.

m) If you are financially rich, and have what you need in your life, do amazing things like buy up the rainforest so that it cannot be used for logging or destroying the habitats of orangutans. Support genius companies cleaning up our oceans of plastic. Protect sea-life, because they need our help. Invest in start-ups doing genius healthy things with food and the environment and natural health. Get involved with organisations that support humanity and bring a wonderful life to those whose lives haven't been wonderful.

Use your money as a force for *good* in this world, and *only* good. You will feel *amazing* and the planet and humanity and animals and people will benefit from this exponentially.

I don't care what any country believes about its borders, we are one world, and one family, and we have to look after each other. How we use our money – and our relationship and beliefs about money – define that.

Finally, get involved in a political or social cause. Be The Change. There is something that only you can do; a difference only you can make.

Remember that you have a purpose, and are here for a reason, and that our world needs you and your courage. We can make the world a better place together. And if at times it seems like it's too hard to do it, remember that the night is ALWAYS darkest before the dawn, but the Light ALWAYS comes, as sure as day follows night. Our world needs us to hold on and shine brightly and Be The Change and that, ultimately, is why I believe you are still here. I believe we will live to see a world of peace in our lifetimes. We just have to hold on for a bit until we get there.

And finally remember that love is – and has always been - the greatest power there is.

Acknowledgements

I am blessed to have some remarkable and wonderful friends in my life, without whom I simply wouldn't be here and still have a modicum of sanity, let alone a sense of humour.

I would like to offer my heartfelt gratitude and thanks to:

Denis Fernando, a brilliant musician and changemaker and fighter for justice, kindness and equality in this world, and two decade long friend and fellow Star Wars fan, who was the first to read this manuscript, and the title of the book is thanks to him. I will forever remember the walk down Regent's Street in London once evening when he gave the most wonderful feedback and showed what true caring friendship really is.

Wendy Prior, aka The Wise Girlfriend, who as well as being a wonderful friend, is a fantastic coach and mentor and inspirer of women around the world, who asked the insightful questions, and shared the wisdom and humour that enabled me to share the lessons I have learned.

Allan Kleynhans who, when he first heard the story, encouraged the book to be finally published in a way I really heard and felt. You are reading this book in part thanks to him.

Some of my closest and dearest friends, Mariana Weigel Munoz, Vickie Simner, Shay Aly, Krish Surroy, Amanda Radix and Sophie Joseph, who every time I publish a book couldn't be more excited and encouraging, and – without realizing it – help me overcome the inner gulp I feel at putting my work out there. I never understood how much courage publishing a book takes, and they help give me my courage.

Some amazing and brilliant soul family and friends, including Joolz Perry, Sarah Leboff, Emma Tuzzio, Helen Shelley, Keri Moss, Lisa O'Connor, Caroline Leon, Inez von Rege, Jenny Kovacs, Mary Dohrmann, Marie Ashton, Gilly Bean, Ann Uddin, Clare Newman, Lucy Setters, Clare Davison, Rachel Murphy, Karima Setohy, Chris Cheeseman, Valeria Rodriguez, Penelope Žikić, Gosia Charyz, Tracy Templeton, Natasha Vladušić, Rachael Beesley, Kate Palmer, Aletheia, Lyla & Juni Gentle, Alpa Pabari, Priya Dey-Ghatak, Shima Bhunjun, Sandra Eriemo, Miche Tetley, Susan Kingdon, Liz Angell, Pooja Agarwal, Jayne & Pat Queen. Thank you all for your wonderful kind and generous friendship, love, encouragement and laughter.

Shara Wajih, Abby Mangold, Ayesha de Silva, Jenny Lightfoot and Marilyn Ragg who were there. I will forever be grateful.

My Mama and my angels who are with me every day, reminding me always that there is more than this life, and to keep laughing whilst living this one. At times laughing at me too, but the with me is wonderful.

My father for helping me learn how to find peace from turmoil.

And my dude, who just is super awesome and cool and wise and brilliant and teaches me the miracle of life and of becoming who we are here to be every day.

About Danica

Danica (pronounced De-nit-sa) is a speaker, writer, blogger, thought leader and health visionary. She is a student homeopath, as well as a training specialist, coach, energy healer, baker and entrepreneur. Her passion is health – for the mind, body, soul, within communities and for our beautiful planet.

Danica has published two other books, The Spiritual Teacher's Handbook and Nature's Medicine Code. She founded The Conscious Cake Company.

She lives in London, England with her son.

www.danicaapolline.co.uk

22744304R00111

Printed in Great Britain
by Amazon